End of the Rainbow

End of the Rainbow

~

Bill Miller

ISBN: 151239047X
ISBN-13: 9781512390476
Library of Congress Control Number: 2015908844
CreateSpace Independent Publishing Platform
North Charleston, South Carolina

Dedication

To the peoples of the world whose wish is to live their lives in peace and harmony with the hope of a better tomorrow.

ACKNOWLEDGMENTS

I acknowledge acceptance of the multicultural diversity of the human race, knowing that every individual is different, yet all are equal.

Contents

CHAPTER 1

THE WAY WE ARE

ARE WE SATISFIED WITH WHAT we are? Do we even know what we are? We think that we do, but the answer is probably no, because if it were yes, it would mean that we just don't give a damn. We talk about how hard it is making a living, but if we have to work to do it, too many would rather stay with the status quo. At the same time, we blame everybody for our inability to pull ourselves up … to get out of the hole that we are in. It's the government's fault, it's due to the economy, the man is trying to keep us down—we have a good reason to explain everything that we fail at doing. We ourselves are the heaviest burden that we carry, yet we keep lumbering along wishing that the load would get lighter.

Instead of beating the pavement looking for a job, too many are content just to sit around all day with a beer in their hands discussing social problems and whatever. Political issues are a favorite, and everybody knows just how to fix them. Those same people won't even take the time to vote in an election. If you don't vote, you probably don't pay much attention to political issues; you probably don't even know what they are.

Anymore, people and places seem to be stuck in neutral. It is very obvious in small towns, because everything is so visible. They used to look like ghost towns during the day, because the streets were almost empty; everybody was at work. Old men and women worked all day long every day to take care of the family. On the weekend—especially on Saturdays—those same towns would come to life with people spending money and taking care of business. Today, those same streets are almost empty every day of the week; the stores are still there, but they are out of business—all except Wall Mart.

During the recession, many of the people in those towns were without a job for a long time. It seems that too many became accustomed to not going to work every day, and now they are satisfied to just get by with what they receive from various state and federal assistance programs. Seeking employment is no longer part of their game plan.

Women use the expression, "my baby's daddy and my other baby's daddy," when they should be referring to them as our children. Yet, she can't refer to them as our children, because the children do not have the same father. Some children grow up not ever knowing who their father is. They don't know, and in some cases the mother's knowledge of her own baby's father is nothing more than her best guess. Having a house full of children without a husband and not being able to properly care for them is not a deterrent to have more children—more kids mean a larger check from the government.

When the mother is asked, "Do you work," too many respond with, "No, not outside the home." When asked, "How do you take care of your children," they're quick to say, "I take good care of all my children." Yet, her response is incorrect, she does not take care of her children; the taxpayers take care of them.

Many people don't know that the assistance they receive is funded with taxpayer dollars. Their benefits are taken from the pockets of those that work, while they sit around doing nothing. They can't understand why the federal government operates in the red—since they own the printing press, why not start it up and print whatever amount of money is needed to satisfy the national debt.

Should it be that simple, then why not print enough money and pass it out so that every person in the country is wealthy. Only then would they realize that starting up the money making machine is not the solution to the problem. Still, it would be of no concern to them.

What about her baby's daddy. He is in the streets, riding around enjoying life and doing whatever—maybe sharing a cold one with his friends. He has enough money to get most of the things that he want—it's money that he gets from his baby's mama … taxpayers' money that she gets to take care of their kids.

It appears as though neither the father nor the mother ever thinks about their children—what will they become when they grow up. Chances are that they will be just like their parents—living in the streets and being supported by their woman that's getting taxpayers money. It is "the life of Riley."

They get food, clothing and housing. They don't get anything for beer, liquor, and the like. However, they can get food at the grocery store and then swap it to get the things that they can't buy. They know how to skirt the prohibitions that come with spending the hard earned money of the working class.

It's not just the people with children that the taxpayers have to support. They have to take care of the disabled as well. The disabled is that bunch that doesn't want to be tied down with supporting a family. Yet, they get a check, because they have a bad back—a bad back that's not a problem when he's in bed grinding away with his woman. It only bothers him when he has to be out among the public.

Older generations can be excused, but not today's generation. There is no excuse for young people not knowing how to read and write effectively. Reading and writing are two of the easiest things to learn in school. They are so simple that every child should know how starting with the first day in the first grade.

Of course, the process of learning becomes more complicated as the student advances—recognizing the fact that some advance because of academic achievement, while others are just passed along to get them out of the school system. There are exceptions, but too many children from single parents go to school just long enough to become of age so that they can drop out.

When they drop out, they become the next generation of moochers on a society that is either too liberal, or too willing to give them just enough to keep them satisfied and uneducated. They can walk the streets and do their thing. No one has to worry about them as long as they don't break any laws, or as long as they don't get caught breaking any laws.

Promoting students from one grade to the next when they have failed to meet the academic requirements is a disservice to the students, a disgrace to the school system and a disgrace to society. It does happen, and sometimes it comes under the heading of subtle racism. A student's report card may show good grades, but the student's level of academic achievement is less than that reflected by his or her grades.

In doing so, the student may enroll in college, because they had good grades in high school. However, they quickly find out that they are not ready for college, which is in direct contrast to the grades on their high school transcript.

It's a subtle form of discrimination that keeps the student from earning a college education. The student and the parents are left disappointed—duped by the school system and those that are part of it with the goal of keeping minorities at the bottom. Neither the parents nor their children ever know what happened, but it does happen.

There are a lot of parents that cannot sit down with their son or daughter and help them with their homework, because the study material is as foreign to them as it is to their children. They cannot afford a tutor, and they may not recognize the fact that their child needs assistance—it's hard to recognize faults in someone else when you have the same unrecognized fault in yourself. Too many students never make it through high school, and they end up on the streets. They have children, and then the cycle repeats itself.

Too many of today's young people are incapable of effectively comprehending and applying proper usage of the English language. When listening to them speak, they seem to be speaking a language other than English—a language that only they and others like them can understand. However, they are speaking English—it's just their version. Those that are fluent in English are the ones that do not understand. Then it is they that need a tutor to help them comprehend, or they need someone to translate.

Whenever you talk to them, you keep saying, "Excuse me, I don't understand what you are saying." Then they say it again, but you still can't get the message. Should you really be in need of getting accurate information from them, you keep asking questions and getting dumb incomprehensible responses. When you finally say, "Thanks," and then walk away, they think that you are an idiot.

When their child fails to make the grade, parents are quick to blame the school system for the students' short comings. The school systems do have problems, but part of the problem is at home and not on campus. If boys and girls spent as much time with their head in a book as they do socializing, then many of the problems at school would go away.

Students that carry handguns and knives to school are not there to get an education. Instead, they are getting an early start on a life of crime. It is not because they decided that such a lifestyle would be best suited for them. It's because they have been misguided, or they had no guidance. As a result, they make the decision to take what they think is the easiest and fastest route to success.

Net worth is the standard most often used to measure success, including those that fall short of academic excellence. Although it is the preferred way, academic excellence is not the only way of affording a lifestyle free of deprivations. However, the less intellectually challenging routes usually lead to the streets of crime.

Those that travel those streets are the uneducated children of parents that failed in their responsibilities. They stood at that fork in the road and watched their sons and daughters go the wrong way. They did it without saying, "Stop." Eventually, their children will become the next generation of stragglers on a system that is already overloaded. Someday, one will be the straw that breaks the camel's back.

All of these scenarios happen, and everybody knows that they do—everybody except those at the top. If they don't know, then they shouldn't be at the top.

There are more problems with the social programs in this country than one can shake a stick at. They are programs that were designed and implemented with good intentions, but they have failed miserably. Every taxpayer in the country knows how much social programs are abused. Yet, the political system keeps on pumping money into them as if they are unaware.

Should welfare programs be an asp slithering around at the State House or on Capitol Hill, every politician in the country would know the sting of fangs, because they would be easy prey.

Likewise, law enforcement officers don't seem to know what's going on in their own backyard. Everybody in town knows the location of every crack house except the police. When you see Joe Blow decked out in the latest threads and riding up and down the streets every day without a job, it should tell you something.

Law enforcement officers seem to be unable to read the signs, or they don't want to read them. Maybe they look the other way, because they don't want to be bothered. Looking the other way seems to have become the norm. It's like no one cares anymore.

When people go to the office of social services, apply for assistance, and then get it, they don't mind putting up an argument if what they get is less than what they expected. Their mindset seems to be that it is owed to them and that it's the government's duty to satisfy their request on demand.

A woman will marry a man that doesn't have anything and no prospects of getting anything. He doesn't have a job, nor does he want one. The only way of supporting themselves is by mooching, but mooching will not last long.

When people figure you out, they cut you lose. Then, their only alternative is to turn to a life of crime, because working is not part of the plan. As a full time job, crime is short lived. It is an occupation that usually ends in death or imprisonment.

Speaking of mooching, what about your good friends and relatives, those that hit you for a loan every now and then—man, can you let me hold four or five hundred dollars until I get my income tax refund. It's strange that a person can get an income tax refund without having a job. When they ask for the money, they always say borrow, but they never repay the loan.

You know that they are not going to pay you back when they ask for it, but you do it anyway. The killer is that they don't pay you back, but they will return at some later date and ask to borrow again. You probably dig into your pocket and hand it over.

When they've suckered you enough, you get fed up and cut them off. That's when they tell everybody that you're a no good son of a bitch. Do they really think that you are the one that is no good? Surely not—they couldn't be that dumb—but on the other hand, maybe they are.

The truth is that people like that don't care about you. In fact, they don't give a damn about you. They just want what they can get without working. When their supply line runs out, they dump you and move on to someone else—they're through with you. They are the monkey on your back and everybody has one. When you cut them loose and move on, at least you have gotten rid of one.

Someday by chance, you will bump into that old friend that you used to loan money to, but he never paid any back. That so called friend is then in a position where they almost have to say something—while staring them in the face, you can see their cheesy grin while they search their twisted mind for the right words. They feel like they have to say something, but they don't know what. You know exactly what they are thinking, but they have no idea as to what's on your mind … theirs is a little slow, it doesn't work like yours.

They are at a loss for words, because they realize for just a short while that they are something less than what they should be. When they do speak, it's obvious that their foot is in their mouth. Still, they're not bothered too much by that, because they're used to it; it's been there before.

Art Linklater used to say, "People are funny." Today, people are crazy—crazy as hell. They would just as soon rob a homeless person and take what little he might have as to help an old lady across the street. They might even rob her if they see a chance of getting away. Whether it's right or wrong is not an issue, if it were, then they would help the old lady across the street and give something to the homeless person.

Young men used to look forward to the day when they were mature enough to move out into the world and pave their own way—make it on their own. They knew that in order to get ahead, they had to leave home, because mama and daddy had already done all that they could do for them. Most of them loved their parents, and they appreciated what they had done for them. Their parents had prepared them for life as best they could—but they had set their sights on something higher than they could ever reach by staying at home.

Young women had the same aspirations as young men. They wanted a good husband, one that they could love and was willing to provide for the family as best he could. They set goals, and made sacrifices so that they might attain those goals. Today, a goal is getting under the basket and making a slam dunk, or hitting a three pointer from downtown on the basketball court.

The young man that used to couldn't wait to leave home and set out on his own stays at home now until he is no longer welcome—still, he will not leave. His parents hope that every day will be his last day in their house unless he is visiting. He sleeps all day and sits around all night using his skilled fingers to tap out messages on his phone.

That same young man can't fill out a job application without someone helping him. If he is not at home, he is with his homies—maybe hanging out someplace where he shouldn't be. That scenario has become a way of life for too many.

The older generation always said aim high. Today's aim would end up shooting someone in the foot. Pride has gone away and been replaced with a chip on the shoulder, and a bad boy attitude.

There was a time when young men might be seen out and about after working hours. Today they are out and about during all hours—holding their phone in one hand and holding their pants up with the other. They can't wave at anyone, because if they do, their pants would end up around their ankles.

Part of the blame for what we have become is without a doubt due to the lucrative assistance programs that are provided by social services to help those in need. Instead of meeting the intended objective, social service offerings have become a system where millions upon millions of dollars could just as well be flushed down the toilet for the good that they do. It's a system that's broken, and the mechanics in Washington, D.C. don't know how to fix it, or they just don't care.

What was intended as assistance to the needy has turned healthy young people into thespians and con artists. As thespians, they have learned to play their role as well as a seasoned Hollywood actor … never missing a cue, always knowing when to grab their cane, and remembering which leg to favor. It's the state and federal government that gets swindled, and it's we the people that pick up the tab while it goes unchecked.

Everybody in town knows what's happening—where their tax dollars are going—but no one blows the whistle; if they did, who would listen? However, there's no need to blow the whistle, because it's impossible for our elected officials to be so naive. They have to know about the sleaze balls, scams, and rip-offs that take place with social services. If they don't know, then they are too in the dark to serve the people that elected them.

Consequently, social service offerings, including food, housing, medical care, and whatever else comes with it has made people lazy. They are lazy to the point that they have no desire to work nor do they have the need. The giveaway's provided by the government equals and sometimes exceeds what they would earn if they were out working—especially if working for minimum wages.

The minimum wage is exactly what most would earn, because they don't have enough education to qualify themselves for a higher paying position. Furthermore, a person must sweat in order to climb the ladder of success. Yet, why sweat when you can sit under a shade tree and wait for that dependable social service handout that arrives on the first of each month.

Everybody on the planet acts as if they are angry. Whenever it seems like the road ahead is beginning to smooth out, we hit a giant pothole that brings things to a halt. One has to wonder if this is the way it has always been, and we just didn't know about it, and now we are more aware, because nothing can be hidden from us anymore.

Whatever the reason, it's very shattering and depressing that after all these years we have what seems to be a need to hate and fight like wild animals. We see anger and aggression all around us every day; we fail to pinpoint the cause so we blame everybody—everybody except ourselves.

We are all guilty of letting things get so out of control. It didn't sneak up on us; we have been seeing the signs all along. We didn't nip it in the bud, and now it has become a mountain that is almost too high to climb.

Although a lot of things are in disrepair, they can still be fixed. First, however, we must have better mechanics and hold them accountable. Congress is not a place for politicians to filibuster and pussyfoot around with taxpayers' money any more than welfare is a place for John Q Public to get a disability check when he is as healthy as an ox. That is the way we are. Yet, we could change it, and then refer to it as, "the way we used to be."

CHAPTER 2

THINK FIRST

BLACK PEOPLE TAKE TO THE streets in protest more than White people. The reason is that Blacks are discriminated against more than Whites. Whenever it appears that the system has failed, we still have to talk to settle our differences rather than taking the law into our own hands and acting like a mob. We shouldn't have the attitude that we are not going to talk anymore, because no one listens.

People do listen; all of them may not, but some do. Whenever there's a large group marching or protesting, look at the people in the crowd—it's a mix of races walking side by side. The ratio may not be as diverse as you would like for it to be, yet it is diverse.

Among the crowd of people, those that are different from you, are those that have heard your plea, and they support your cause. They are there, because they too have recognized that the scales of justice are sometimes off center and need to be balanced; they want to help balance them, so that we all stand on common grounds. All the while, we must be mindful of the fact that bloodshed and fear will not pave the way for a better tomorrow.

Citizens in this country—the United States of America—have the right of peaceful assembly, to protest what they consider to be unfair or unjust treatment. They can legally come together in masses to express their grievances and bring attention to their cause—whatever it may be. However, when protesters resort to destroying property and/or disobeying the laws for whatever reason, then they are committing a crime.

The general public is more likely to sympathize with a cause when it is a peaceful protest rather than a disorderly mob rioting in the streets. Many sympathizers and would be sympathizers will turn their backs when protesters get wild and overly aggressive. Some will even begin to think that the stigma already stuck on Black people is more real rather than a stereotypical labeling.

After the town has been destroyed, whatever it is that they are fighting for had better be a hot and obvious miscarriage of justice. Otherwise, when the debris has been cleaned up and the smoke has settled, their cause will be back at square one and with far less support than when they started.

Black people are quick—too quick at times—to take to the streets in protest of unfair treatment. They do it without having a clear understanding of the facts, what happened and why. Every Black person that is killed by a police officer is not innocent, and every police officer that shoots a Black person is not a killer cop.

Should Blacks overreact, they feel justified in doing so, because they have come to believe that sitting at the table discussing their grievances is a lost cause before the discussions begin. They feel that way, because they have been lied to and mistreated too long and by too many. Still, the first move is to get a clear understanding of the facts, not hearsay, but the facts, rather than taking to the streets on a gut feeling.

If you are not Black, you may think that you understand the plight of Black people, but you do not. You don't understand and you don't know their feelings unless you are one of them. Every civil liberty that Blacks have today had to be earned through bloodshed and death. Even then, the civil liberties that have been granted are not entirely theirs to hold. Although they are eloquently worded statutes, sometimes they are little more that empty promises that are carved in stone.

White people can make a somewhat similar claim. They had to fight and die to earn independence. Although they fought and died, the arena is all different. Blacks had to do it in their country of citizenship, and they had to do it simply because, they are Black.

If you are Black, it's easy to become angry about how the system operates, because it is undoubtedly one sided. Although pleas for fairness in the quest for human rights sometimes fall on deaf ears, resolutions must still follow the course of legal procedures in the pursuit of justice. When it seems that no one is listening, then is the time to speak louder, but it must be done within the confines of the legal system.

The social media are good at keeping people agitated and maintaining a wide gap between Whites and Blacks. Someone is always standing by, willing and ready, to post something on Facebook about the mistreatment of Blacks—old photos of Blacks being lynched, burned alive, or flogged mercilessly. It happens, and the frequency increases whenever there are heated flare-ups regarding White and Black issues.

Such postings fuel the flames of hatred as if their intent is to make sure that Black people stay angry or become more angry. There is nothing wrong with anger. However, something is wrong when anger becomes an uncontrollable madness.

Too many are too quick to see something posted or printed by the media, especially the social media, and take it at face value, when much of it can be discarded as hogwash or just plain garbage. Via the social media, what starts out as an intelligent exchange about racial issues quickly turns into a war of words with all parties refusing to back off or cede anything. The only barrier that keeps them from going at each other's throat is the distance between them.

We sit and watch the news on television and almost half of what we hear is opinions rather than facts. Reporting reflects the position and the opinion that station management has on the issues. When it comes to politics, some stations favor the Republican Party while others favor the Democrat Party, and it is all very obvious. It is also obvious that the darkest side of Black people—catching them at their worst—is a favorite of the news media.

Black people believe that Fox News reporting is far more biased toward Blacks than CNN News. When the listeners think that they are getting accurate information based on facts, it might be nothing more than their opinions presented as facts. The same is true for newspapers.

Biased news reports or reporting falsified information is no better than no news at all. In fact, it probably does more harm than good. That is, unless your job is to keep the television station or newspaper ratings up. The news media will feed anything to the public if it meets their agenda. While they dish it out, it's taken in as if it's the gospel.

CHAPTER 3

A World of Hate

We should stop teaching our children to be racists so that they grow up to be better men and women than we are. Sometimes it appears as though the country is heading toward another civil war.

Too many of us have the, "I don't care attitude." We don't have to care, but things would be much better if we would. If we don't care about what we represent, about the things around us, and about how we are perceived by others, then we are nothing more than a drag on ourselves, and on society. When we don't care about ourselves, we shouldn't expect anyone else to be overly concerned.

It probably comes under the heading of resentment born of pride—a quality that can sometimes become a stumbling block. Whenever the system by which the people are governed is one sided, then the people should be angry. However, directing anger and aggression toward an entire race of people based on what some have done is not right. It is not right, because some of them stand with you, and they support your cause.

It's difficult to understand why a person dislikes another person just because of their color. Most Black people will say that they dislike White people because they held their ancestors as slaves. Slavery ended with the Civil War—about one hundred and fifty years back. All slave owners have long since been dead and gone to wherever slave owners go.

No one in their right mind can deny that slavery was wrong, but hating every successive generation of White people since way back then is a long time to hate. Furthermore, most of them didn't own a single slave. Yet, we keep on hating because of what someone else did.

Look deeper into the idea that Black people hate White people today, because they enslaved the ancestors of Black people; then consider how slaves got to America in the first place. The Black people that were brought to this country and sold into slavery were first sold to slave traders by other Black people. Payment included such meager items as pieces of metal, pots, cloth, beads and trinkets and the like.

It is a well-known fact that Blacks were sold into slavery by their own people. Is a paradigm shift like that sufficient reason to reconsider the thought process of whom we hate and why? In no way are these facts presented to excuse White people in this country or any other country for their role in slavery.

The terrible things that White people did to Blacks during the era of slavery were done deliberately and they were wrong. However, these facts are intended to at least make Black people wonder about the harbored hatred that has become a cancer—gnawing at us until we become unmindful of our thoughts and uncaring about the things that we do.

White people also have their reasons for not being overly fond of Black people—they don't understand us, we're lazy, uneducated, ignorant, etc.—none of which makes any sense. Most Black people probably do believe that White people's hate for Blacks go back to slavery. They believe that Whites have been angry since slavery was abolished, because they wanted to preserve a way of life that had placed them in a superior position. They were lord and master over what they considered an inferior race. Whites also lost a source of hand labor that was the driving force behind a thriving economy.

Slavery cannot be dismissed as a reason for the hate that exists today between the two races. However, a more recent event still festering and being fostered in the minds of both Black and White people may be what keeps hate alive—the civil rights movement and the subsequent Civil Rights Act of 1964.

There are many people living today that remember and were part of the struggle for civil rights in the 1960's. They still remember the indecencies imposed on them by Whites for simply exercising their inalienable rights as citizens of this country—rights that were too long in coming, rights that required too much bloodshed, and rights that took too many lives after enactment to be recognized.

White people also still remember. They remember being defeated by their own government that sided with Blacks against the will of the White majority. It was a coup de' grace that would put an end to White rule.

Both Black and White people that remember and took part in the civil rights movement of the 1960's, and even those that stood on the sidelines and watched will soon become dust. Yet, amongst our ranks are some that have preached so long and so hard about racial hatred that it cannot die. Instead, they keep it alive and well in the minds of those that will listen.

They have sought to preserve and nurture an infectious disease that should have been eradicated long ago. Should it be true that today's racial tensions were born from the race riots of the 1960's, will tomorrow's racial tensions be the unwanted progeny of today's unrest.

None of us, regardless of color, have a reason to keep on hating and hurting from now until forever. We can't forget the past—it will always be there, and when we look back we will see it. Yet, we should recognize it for what it was and then let it go.

Instead of parading in the streets, breaking windows, and throwing Molotov cocktails, let us walk those same streets—arms locked with one another regardless of race, creed, or color—and have an annual worldwide day celebrating peace and goodwill to all. It would be so easy to do, yet it is something that will never be done … just weightless words and useless efforts that drift away like dust in the wind.

Black people and White people should be the same, except for color. Should you happen to be one of those that are the progeny of both races, sometimes you feel like an outcast, scrutinized by both Whites and Blacks and wondering what they think of you. You are too White for one race and too Black for the other. Then where do you go?

Of late, it seems that White people are on the rampage with hate and more so than Blacks. Not implying that the number of White racists is on the increase, but meaning that White people seem to have kicked things up a notch by getting out into the open with it more than in the past. Instead of keeping it a closed conversation within their own circles, they have now taken it to the airways with an in the face attitude so that the world can see.

Wayne LA Pierre Jr. is an advocate of the right to bear arms. During a speech at the National Rifle Association's meeting, he said, "Eight years of one demographically symbolic president is enough." What he said is nothing more than a jacked up in the face of Black people way of saying, "Having to put up with a Black President for eight years is all that I can stand." He didn't stop there. He let it be known that a White woman—probably referencing Hillary Clinton—wouldn't be any better. Black women were probably covered in his statement, "Eight years of one demographically … ."

It is very surprising to see so many of today's young White people being so overt with their expressions of racial hatred. In the past, it was the older generation that was most open and most outspoken. The general hope and belief has been that today's young White and Black people would heal the wounds that were inflicted by the generations before them. Maybe they will, but without change, who will heal the wounds that they make? Perhaps it will be deferred until the next generation, or the next … and maybe never?

At its' worst, our feelings toward someone with whom we are not acquainted should be neutral, because we have not experienced anything to make us feel otherwise. The only way that a friendship can develop from that neutral feeling is that it be cultivated. Should hatred develop, then it too must be cultivated. However we feel about another person—whether it be positive or negative—can only be sustained by nourishing our own thoughts.

Too many White people judge other Black people based on the actions of a few. They see a few Blacks doing wrong and then categorize too many others as being the same. Too many Black people think that all White people are the same just because they're White. Nothing could be further from the truth.

White people will visit Blacks when they are sick. They don't stop by to see how long it might be before the

Black person die's so that they can remove another name from their list. Instead, they stop by to show that they care. Black people do the same thing with Whites.

White people attend Black funerals to let the family of the deceased know that they share their grief. If they didn't care, they wouldn't be there. They could pick up a newspaper or get it from word of mouth that the person is dead. In other words, they didn't attend the funeral just to make sure that what they had heard is true.

If a person is White, yet they do not have many Black friends, it is probably because they have chosen to segregate themselves from Black people. Turn it around and the same thing is true. If a Black person does not have many White friends, then that person is probably a segregationist as well.

The thing that is wrong is that we distance ourselves from the other race, and it is something that we ourselves have chosen to do. Should a person be a racist or should they not be, is expressed by their actions—the things that they do or fail to do.

We live in a multicolored, multicultural world, and it is alright with most of us. Yet, too many Whites in America seem to believe that the number of no good Blacks is far greater than the number of good Blacks. Black people believe the same thing about Whites. It is probably next to impossible to change those beliefs. If those erroneous stigmas do not change, then whatever America is today is what she will be for a long time to come—maybe forever.

CHAPTER 4

ARE YOU A RACIST

WE HAVE RACISM AND PREJUDICE; both words are oftentimes used in the same context, but sometimes they do have different meanings. Racism is the learned belief that one race is superior to another. Prejudice is the prejudging of a situation or a person in the absence of facts, or rational thought processes—making an assumption and then coming to a conclusion with nothing to verify.

Racism is always bad, but prejudice may or may not be. Everyone is guilty of making decisions without knowing the facts. Should a person say, "Never in my life have I eaten a rattlesnake, and I never will," then that person is being prejudice.

The person is only guilty of making a preconceived judgment based on the fear of eating a well battered, deep fried poisonous reptile without ever tasting. Although it tastes just like chicken, no harm is done. At the same time, we can be prejudiced toward people just because we do not know them and they look different.

A racist is always aware of the fact that they are a racist. Most of the time when speaking of people and we use the word prejudice, it's used to imply a dislike for someone of another race. In doing so, the word prejudice takes on the same meaning as racism.

Should a person have to ask, "Am I prejudiced," or, "Am I a racist," then they probably are, otherwise there would be no need to ask the question. The answer cannot be, "Maybe I'm a little prejudiced," or, "Maybe I'm somewhat of a racist," because neither prejudice nor racism comes with varying degrees. It's very simple, "is you is, or is you ain't." There is no rating scale, and there are only two possible answers, "yes or no."

Many White people do not believe that they are prejudiced. They see themselves as being open minded and recognizing all people as being equal, regardless of color. However, you may still be prejudice, even though you do not use the n word, and you have never participated in a lynching.

A simple thing like not asking your Black neighbor or friend to attend church with you on Sunday might be because you do not want that person in your church. You may not care about them being in your home, but you are careful about where you are seen with them in public. Your concern is, what others will think if they see you sitting in church next to a Black person that you invited.

You associate with people that do not want to associate with Blacks. At the same time, you are satisfying your prejudice friends while forsaking your Black friend. You attend church on Sunday and serve God, because you are a Christian. It would be Godlier to attend a church where your Black friend is welcomed rather than a church where he is banned. Are you still a Christian should you do otherwise? In a way, you are being prejudiced.

Most of us will stand up and tell the world that we're not prejudiced. Yet, in any competition—sports, politics, whatever—do you find yourself rooting for the person that is your favorite just because they're your favorite, or do you root for the person that looks most like you … the person whose skin most closely matches the color of yours.

Black people can ask themselves whether or not they voted for Barack Obama, because they felt like he was most qualified for the job, or did they vote for him simply because he is Black, and his opponent was White. White people can ask whether or not they voted for Mitt Romney, because they felt like he was most qualified for the job, or was it because he is White, and his opponent was Black.

If Barack Obama was White and Mitt Romney was Black, and that was the only thing different, the outcome of the election would certainly have been different. Both candidates maintaining their political platforms and their spiritual beliefs, but switching the color of their skin—should it be possible—would have been the deciding factor on how America would have voted.

Opinions on the other side of the aisle would be flip-flopped. Donald Trump would not have made the offer to pay five million dollars to Barack Obama's favorite charity just to see his college transcript and passport records. President Obama's birth records would not have been suspect. Obama health care reform would have swept the nation and been viewed as the best thing since the New Deal.

Most people will hedge on expressing their own true thoughts about racism, especially in public. They try to give the impression that race does not matter, and they don't care about the color of a person's skin.

A professional person—especially one whose career hinges on public acceptance and approval—must stand in front of the camera and willingly tell the world that diversity is the cornerstone of democracy. At the same time, that person might be the best definition of racism in town.

Not everyone has to be so careful with their opinions and thoughts about race relations. They can say whatever and shout as loudly as possible to make sure that they are heard. They can do it, because they are the blowhard scatterbrain that no one pays attention to.

Whenever two people approach each other on the streets—complete strangers—they can tell before they meet whether or not they should say hello. They can tell by the other's body language as they approach each other. Some can strike up a friendly conversation in a crowd with a person that they don't even know. They can look at each other and tell whether or not the other is approachable and if they might want to talk.

We have a learned self-taught ability—one that we usually exercise unconsciously—that allows us to determine some things about another person's character without speaking. It is an ability that some can employ effectively, while others are either incapable of interpreting what they see, or they just don't try because they're too resentful.

Black people don't usually think of themselves as being prejudiced or racist toward Whites. Instead, they think of themselves as being the victims. When it comes to racism, Blacks are no different from Whites. We just fail to recognize that we are not different.

Some Blacks may even think that prejudice and racist are terms used exclusively by Blacks and reserved specifically for them to refer to White people. However, racism is as prevalent within one race as it is the other. We are all just alike.

Suppose that one hundred households are chosen at random; each household has the television set tuned in to the tennis channel watching Serena Williams and Eugenie Bouchard go at it. Many Whites would be pulling for Eugenie Bouchard, and many would support Serena Williams. However, all Blacks would favor Serena Williams. If you don't think so, then watch them go against each other sometimes, and then pay attention to which one you're rooting for.

Eugenie Bouchard is a White Canadian, and Serena Williams is an African American. Bouchard would be "The Great White Hope" of White racists, and they would not care which country she call's home. The only thing that would matter is that she is White. Serena

Williams is always the favorite among Blacks in America simply because she is Black.

Should a Black woman from any other country—a foreigner—be pitted against a White player from the United states, then African Americans would root for the Black foreigner rather than the White person, even though she would be an American citizen. Blacks would do it, because they do not want to cheer for a White person when they have a choice.

That's exactly the way we are, and it's exactly what we need to get away from. We should stop making decisions, stop liking, and stop disliking based on the color of a person's skin.

If God made an error, maybe it was giving us eyes so that we can see. We would all have some other sense organ to find our way around. Should He ever decide to do it one more time, those that He blow His breath of life into will not be able to distinguish night from day.

A Black person rooting for Serena Williams and a White person rooting for Eugenie Bouchard, does not necessarily mean that they are a racist. They could be showing favoritism. One definition of favoritism is the unfair practice of treating some people better than others. Synonyms include prejudice, bias, inequality, unfairness and discrimination. By definition, favoritism sounds a lot like racism, but is it wrong if a person opts to cheer for the person of their race rather than the person of another race?

Should White people prefer being among other White people, does that make them racists? Conversely, should Black people prefer hanging out with other Blacks, are they racists? Those preferences could be due to the fact that our minds have been preconditioned to perceive and accept, i.e., Favor that which we have been exposed to the most.

In other words, we are more comfortable in the environment that we have come to know. Yet, many of those same people have no problem with stepping across to the other side and mixing with those of a different race. They do it willingly and unconsciously.

If there is a fault with the environment that we have come to know—the place where we are most comfortable—then it is the lack of diversity. Yet, the lack of diversity in our immediate surroundings does not necessarily mean that we are racists. It could be just a reflection of the remnants still lingering from the past that put us where we are today. Remnants that are not rooted in hatred, yet they are old habits that are slow to go away, because we are creatures of habit.

Consequently, a Black person rooting for Serena Williams in a tennis match and a White person rooting for Eugenie Bouchard may or may not be exhibiting racial discrimination or racial prejudice. Although they favor the person of their own race, it might be a subconscious no harm intended expression of the environment in which we live.

America has had its' Great White Hope's. They were early twentieth century boxing matches where White people in the United States cheered for any White man from any country in the world with the hope of him defeating Black champions like Jack Johnson and Joe Louis.

There are always exceptions, even to the Great White Hope. In the United States, the home crowd is overwhelmingly White at all professional tennis matches. Yet, the home crowd always supports their own, regardless of color.

Still, it sounds like a very narrow line separates favoritism from discrimination, but favorites are something that we all have and always will. Apple pie and ice cream are America's favorites, but a slice of German chocolate is just as good. Maybe the day will come when we will be willing to step outside our comfort zone and explore that part of humanity which we have never let ourselves come to know.

I do not support the death penalty, because I know how our system operates. The system is far from being balanced, and the scales of justice are tilted in favor of White people. Race of the victim and race of the defendant are major factors in determining the degree of punishment.

White people have been found guilty and wrongly executed for committing capital crimes of which they were innocent, and so have Black people, but to a greater extent. However, a Black person murdering a White person is more likely to receive the maximum penalty than a White person is that murder's a Black person.

In those states where capital crimes are punishable by death, should the person be guilty, then waiting to be executed for a crime has to be torturous—sitting in a jail cell—first counting days, then hours, and then minutes. However, that person committed the crime, and according to the laws in that state, that person must pay the ultimate price.

If the person is innocent, then the way that they feel is undoubtedly unimaginable … being executed for a crime that was committed by someone else. Yet, it has happened many times, and the first time was one too many.

The State of South Carolina executed George Stinney, a fourteen year old Black kid in 1944. He was strapped in the electric chair and killed with nothing more than circumstantial evidence. His parents were forced to leave town or face a lynch mob—possibly one of the biggest miscarriages of justice ever handed down. When it was over, no one cared much about what had happened, simply because, George Stinney was Black.

On Monday, December 15, 2014, a University of Pennsylvania fraternity apologized after posing for a holiday picture with a Black blow-up doll ... a racist prank. Phi Delta Theta's photo appeared on social media Sunday—the day before issuing the apology—showing twenty nine members of the mostly White Ivy League school with smiles on their faces. An apology should not have been necessary, because it was something that should have never happened.

Just when this country is experiencing so much racial unrest, the supposedly elite ivy leaguers felt the need to jack things up even more. Society would not suffer greatly if they were expelled from school. The biggest loss would be in the form of tuition for the University of Pennsylvania.

If Phi Delta Theta's twenty nine were expelled from school, the school would lose tuition from those students. However, the school would make it up with increased enrollment when other potential students see that the University of Pennsylvania did the right thing. In addition, there would be other students attending the University of Pennsylvania rather than changing schools after seeing Phi Delta Theta students practicing racism on campus. Some would leave, because not all White people are racists, and we should stop assuming that they are.

If a person is intelligent enough to attend college, they should have enough sense to realize the consequences of their actions beforehand. Yet, twenty nine students at the University of Pennsylvania posed for the camera so that they could post a visual racial slur on the social media, and not one said, "No, this isn't right."

Prior to posting their photo, they could have read Article 19 of The Universal Declaration of Human Rights regarding freedom of expression. If they did, they chose to ignore the part about being respectful of the rights of others. On the other hand, if they did read it, maybe they were unable to interpret its full meaning. Whatever the case, any dumbbell should have known not to do such a thing—not then or ever.

Shortly, after Phi Delta Theta did their thing at the University of Pennsylvania, a fraternity at the University of Oklahoma had to do theirs. Several White students of Sigma Alpha Epsilon were captured on video singing a racist song—one that they had composed—while riding on a bus. Everybody on the bus was White, yet someone on the bus posted the video online.

The person that posted the video could have kept it hidden. However, that person chose to do the right thing, even when no one was looking. It was the right thing to do, because it reinforced the fact that a sarcastic display of that nature is unacceptable to both White and Black people.

Those that participated in the racial chant are the young leaders of tomorrow, but leaders that only a fool would follow. People like that should wear a prophylactic at all times, because they breed racism—they are the fathers of an unwanted yet too often begotten offspring that the world can do without.

Being a racist has no benefits other than perhaps self-satisfaction, and to be so inclined is by choice. Racism may be a social disease of the mind that is contagious and transmitted by being in close contact with others. Certainly, it is a plague; it should be eradicated or at least quarantine the carriers. It has cursed humanity since the middle ages, and it may be a plague that will be a curse until the end of time.

On the internet, or in old newspapers, one can find old photographs of Blacks that were lynched by Whites. If you look closely, most of the time there are a few onlookers in the crowd with smiles on their faces—posing for the camera after committing murder. In doing so, they are as despicable as the crime that they participated in. If they stood there and watched, then they too are guilty.

Of recent, it seems that more White racists have decided to jack things up and go public—unable to hold it inside any longer. There are more social media sites filled with racial comments than one can imagine, and certainly they contain more filth than one wants to read. For sure, there are similar sites filled with similar racist remarks by Black people. Yet, White people seem to be winning in the race of publicizing hate messages, if indeed it is a race that anyone wants to win.

CHAPTER 5

Our Needs are the Same

The Civil War marked the end of slavery. Yet, slavery is something that should have never happened—everybody knows that. Anyone, then or now that tried or tries to justify slavery is a damned fool. Anyone who thinks that Blacks were set free when the war ended have been misinformed. The Civil War let former slaves walk away from the plantation for a while and then return to the same hell hole that they were in before the war started. They went back because they had no other place to go.

Although most former slaves went back to the cotton fields as free people, not much changed except the name. Instead of being slaves, they were referred to as sharecroppers—sharecroppers without a share. The same log cabin with cracks in the wall and a dirt floor that used to be home was once again theirs. Most people don't realize it, but most Southern Blacks did not get away from the forced substandard accommodations of working in the fields from sun up to sundown, with little or no pay, until toward the end of the 1960's.

As sharecroppers, they put in six long days every week. When it was too cold or too wet to work outside, the boss man would find something else for them to do, e.g., sitting in the barn husking corn, or cleaning out the stables.

They had to do whatever they were told without questioning. Failure to do so would result in suffering through the embarrassment of being cursed or kicked in public or in front of their family while maintaining a submissive attitude.

Today, when speaking of racial equality, sooner or later the conversation will get to the part about how much progress Black people have made since slavery. One must concede that in spite of continued abuse and unfair treatment, life for Black people is nothing close to what it was like during slavery; it's nothing close to what it was like fifty or sixty years ago. At the same time, it should also be understood that Jim Crow didn't die until sometime during the 1960's. Although he died, his ghost still haunts us, and his deeds are sometimes shrouded by the best democracy on earth.

In the last one hundred years, a lot of wrongs have been righted—things that have been fixed are too numerous to mention. Most of the fixer uppers were done to comply with state and federal laws. However, the others are more meaningful, because they were done simply because it was the right thing to do—they were done without coercion. The Civil Rights Act of 1964, and the Voting Rights Act of 1965 should have never been necessary. They should have been understood and already granted as inalienable rights guaranteed to all.

In 2008, the United States House of Representatives apologized to African Americans for slavery and racial discrimination. In 2009, the United States Senate did the same thing. It took almost one hundred and fifty years after the signing of the Emancipation Proclamation to say, "We're sorry." That's too long to admit that you were wrong. It wasn't just African Americans that were due an apology—apologizes were made to the Native Americans, and Japanese Americans as well.

When considering African Americans, Native Americans and Japanese Americans, which group ended up with the short straw? It seems as though the Native Americans may have been hit the hardest. This country was theirs, but it was invaded by Europeans. After settling in, the early settlers eventually started a campaign to exterminate Native Americans by whatever means possible—murder, starvation, disease—it didn't matter. The motto was, "The only good Indian is a dead Indian."

When they could no longer fight to defend what was theirs, Native Americans were forced onto reservations. The reservation was nothing more than a prison with invisible walls. It was a place to live and die a slow death while being cared for by a government that didn't care whether they lived or died. The latter was probably preferred.

Had the campaign against Native Americans been severe enough to completely wipe out the entire population, then who would the code talkers have been? The United States military used Native Americans to transmit coded messages back and forth during the world wars. Using their native language, the messages could be intercepted by the enemy, but they could not be decoded, because it was a language that no others could understand.

It was an ingenious tactic executed by a people that were hardly recognized for their contributions when the war ended. It goes without saying that they helped win the war. However, we can only speculate as to what the war would have been like or what the outcome might have been without them.

During World War II, about 120,000 Japanese Americans were placed in confinement camps after the bombing of Pearl Harbor by Imperial Japan. In 1988, President Ronald Regan signed into law the Civil Liberties Act, which basically said that we are sorry and we apologize. Each confinement camp survivor and their heirs were compensated with a payment of $20,000.

The Native Americans finally got something in the form of a payment for the government's shady dealings and even their aboveboard, yet unethical exploitations. Without a doubt, any payment that was made was inadequate. Yet, they did see fit to do something.

The government took this country and slaughtered any Native Americans that fought back. Some didn't fight back, but they were slaughtered anyway—it was easy pickings. Therefore, what constitutes a fair and just settlement? It would be an amount that the government does not have. Should Bernie Madoff be put in charge of raising funds for an equitable settlement, it would be more than even he could handle.

So why didn't the descendants of former slaves—African Americans—get their slice of the pie? Each Japanese American and their heirs received $20,000 for being detained over a period of about three years. If the same act was applied to slaves and their heirs, it would span a period of about four hundred years. Trying to put together a package deal for a fair settlement would be the damnedest undertaking ever.

Instead of making a fair and equitable monetary offering, it would be cheaper and easier to just turn the entire country over to the descendants of former slaves. However, any African Americans sitting around waiting for their slice of the pie can forget it—the pie is all gone, and you'll have to eat cake. The exploitation of our forefathers hundreds of years ago doesn't mean a thing anymore.

Black people believe that White people are responsible for the problems that we have with race relations. Conversely, White people believe the opposite—that Blacks are the problem. One thing that both races agree on is that there is a problem.

The problem is all of us. We can't stop lambasting and pointing a finger at each other. Instead, we keep adding fuel to the fires of hatred when we should be dousing the flames with kindness while getting to know each other. The good things that we talk about doing come nowhere close to the things that we actually do.

What is it anyway about the color of a person's skin that sends up a red flag? Are we afraid of each other? We shouldn't be, because we see all colors of people every day, and we should be accustomed to each other by now.

The scene is too common; walk into a crowded room and see mostly Blacks on one side and Whites on the other. Instead of segregating ourselves so that the picture in front of us is like a chocolate cake with White frosting, we should blend together and look like a well-mixed container of salt and pepper. Yet, it is not like that, because we are all too reluctant to move away from our own kind. It's like we are afraid.

Some of us refuse to mingle, because we do not want to be near the other race. Then there are those that keep their distance unconsciously. They do it simply because that's the way it has always been.

White people sometimes wonder why it is that Blacks can refer to other Blacks as a nigger, and no one is offended. Yet, that same Black person resents being called a nigger by a White person. Blacks do commonly refer to other members of the Black race as a nigger, but it's a term that is used only when speaking with a close friend or when angry. It is ironic that both instances of usage are at the opposing ends of human emotions.

Whether or not it is acceptable to use the word nigger in movies had to be debated. Movie makers claim that it should be acceptable, because it represents reality, and thereby adds authenticity in their attempt to create a true to life production. Furthermore, they argue that they have the right to use the word and that right is supported by the First Amendment to the United States Constitution. Naysayers argue that using the word nigger in movies is derogatory and thereby should be banned.

Both arguments—for and against—are probably true to some extent, or at least have some merit. However, the success or failure of a movie cannot and does not hinge on the use of just a single word. Defending its' usage based on the United States Constitution is no good. Good common sense should tell any rational minded person to erase it from their vocabulary and forget it, because it's not worth remembering.

It is understood among Blacks that the word nigger has two connotations, but only one among Whites. On the other hand, some Whites—especially the younger generation—have the liberty to refer to a close Black friend as nigger without any provocations. Should there be any doubt about where one's position is in another person's circle, it's best not to use the word at all. Reality is that there are no appropriate circumstances where the term should be acceptable.

In a 2013 interview with YouTube personality, Jan Helfeld, Dr. Ben Carson, Pediatric Neurosurgeon, retired, said that the Congressional Black Caucus is essentially acting in a racist fashion by not allowing non Blacks to join. Immediately, some Blacks referred to Carson as being an Uncle Tom and as being stupid.

Membership in the Congressional Black Caucus is limited only to African Americans. If Ben Carson is an uncle tom and stupid, then he is not alone. Any rational minded person should realize that it is wrong.

The National Association for the Advancement of Colored People (NAACP) has an open membership.

Anyone that believes in civil rights for everybody can join. However, the name is like that of the Congressional Black Caucus—symbolic of racism.

Should we have a group created and given the name, National Association for the Advancement of White people, or the Congressional White Caucus, the country would be in an uproar to say the least. The argument for justification by Black leaders goes something like, "Black people need an advocate, a group with enough political influence to help ensure fair treatment and equal rights."

No truer words have ever been spoken. However, it is still time for a name change. Whenever it is alright for one race of people to do something, but restrictions are placed on another, it is not alright. It is a double standard regardless of how we look at it, and it cannot be reasonably justified.

Of all places, double standards should not be allowed to take root and grow in a democracy founded on the precept of equal rights for all. Double standards are the reason why Blacks are upset now, so do away with it. Black politicians in Washington, D.C. should be leading the charge.

No one can possibly believe that Black people wouldn't tear down the town should White people create groups with names like the aforementioned two—save the KKK. Every Black person that can walk would have a wrecking bar in their hands walking the streets looking for something to pry loose. They would do it, because it would be a blatant display of racism, and racism is sickening.

If what White people can do comes with limitations, then those same limitations should apply to Blacks. A people cannot live together in harmony unless they are all bound by the same rules and regulations. Sometimes it seems as though we really do have two sets of rules—the time was when we did for sure—but not today. Sometimes the rules are obviously bent, and sometimes they are concealed and deviously applied, but we should all still live by the same rules.

We still have too many amongst us that are resistant to change, and a few of them are able to keep on getting themselves placed in positions of authority. They are stuck in the past and refuse to evolve with a changing world—supporting a used to be Jim Crow that is too weak to support himself. The rules and the laws that we are governed by are good. We just need to get rid of a few bad apples.

The justice system in the United States is designed to represent all citizens without bias. Unfortunately, we have multiple systems in this country, one for Blacks vs Whites, one for Blacks vs Blacks, one for Whites vs Whites, and one for the rich and famous. It sounds like a joke, but we do have those systems. However, they are not described in any books of law, but they are well understood and too often sanctioned.

No one can intelligently argue the fact that Blacks are not targeted by law enforcement officers. In November, 2014, Brad Heath, Investigative Reporter, USA Today, reported that seventy law enforcement departments across the country arrested Black people at a rate ten times higher than non-Blacks.

He ceded that the disproportional number of arrests could be due to a number of underlying factors such as discrimination by law enforcement officers, and or economic and educational differences across the country—all of which are related to the incidence of crime. Regardless, the fact remains that Blacks are targeted.

After being arrested, Blacks are walked on again in the courtrooms. According to the United States Sentencing Commission, Black men serve about twenty percent longer prison terms than White men for the same crime. It all happens in a country that guarantees equal justice for all—yet, some can see a footnote at the bottom of the page that reads, "except for Black people, and a few Whites."

The laws by which we are governed must be administered fairly and enforced without bias. Otherwise, the friction that exists between the races of man will not die, but will be sustained and nourished by hate and vengeance.

The problems that we have today are the results of our own faults and our unwillingness to let go of the past. None of us can undo what has already happened, but we can do some repair work, and we can make sure that it never happens again. Racism and hatred are major problems—perhaps as major as any problem that the world has ever had—putting an end to it could perhaps be the easiest thing that the world has ever done.

Ending racism, hatred, and the inequalities that come with it would not require an assembly of world leaders, no monetary investment, and no words of wisdom from the wise. It would require that all of us flush away the filth in our minds, to open our hearts, and then recognize each other as equals. No venture could possibly yield so much for so little—a handshake and a smile would get it done—but even that is more than we care to invest.

It's impossible to understand the human mind, what makes us tick and what sets us off. We are all so different, not referencing physical makeup or genetics, but our thought processes, behavioral patterns, what we believe in, and why. Most of us don't even pay attention to ourselves, and most of the things that we do are second nature; born of habit and then done instinctively, because we have been a certain way for so long.

A good example is a person getting too far out of line with society's norms, perhaps becoming a fanatic or suffering from mental illness. When they stray, more often than not it's toward wrong doing. It seems that it would be just as easy to drift in the other direction, and move to the positive side—become engrossed with doing something right.

Instead of touting evil and inflicting pain, start a crusade for peace and wellbeing—then so what if you go overboard. But that's never the case. Those that go too far always grab a gun. We can now add hatchets and whatever else they can get their hands on to the list.

It is equally confusing as to how some people, regardless of ethnicity, can become friends and have the same affections for each other as if blood relatives. Their relationship is not influenced by the other's heritage, and their world is in sync.

CHAPTER 6

WHO'S RIGHT AND WHO'S WRONG

Too many people refuse to associate with others because of race, religion, politics, sexual preference—the list goes on and on. There is not much that anyone can do about the color of a person's skin, but a person's religion, their political views, and their sexual preferences should be theirs and theirs alone—they shouldn't matter to anyone else. Right or wrong, it's their decision.

We disrespect the religion of others just because theirs is different from ours. Not only do we disrespect, we are willing to wage wars and kill, because of our religious differences. The attitude is, "should your faith be different from mine, then yours is wrong."

People have the right to agree or to disagree, and that right should be respected. Should those that practice Catholicism believe that theirs is the only true and righteous faith, then they have the right to have that belief. However, it is not incumbent upon them, nor should it be their goal, to force their faith onto others.

Worship whatever you worship. Should what you're doing be wrong and sinful is not for us to decide. Should you believe that God is real, then let Him reckon with who is right and who is wrong. Let Him do it, because we are not capable, nor is it something that we should do.

It is impossible for us to be the judge of who is right and who is wrong, because we get it wrong too many times. We have killed people by mistake, sent people to prison by mistake, and pointed our finger at others by mistake.

There is no margin for error when someone's life is at stake, yet people are wrongfully executed—not to imply that any execution is anything other than wrong—but we have given ourselves the power to judge and then to decide another's fate just because we have chosen to do so.

Should the power to judge, condemn, and execute be granted by religious freedoms, or interpreted as such, then what good is religion. It is not worth the time it takes to go to church on Sunday? Is it worth anything?

A religious faith that is meant to be the cornerstone for humanity, to foster love and understanding, and give mankind a superior being to believe in and trust—whether it be real or unreal—when all else fails has become Satan's playground.

Politicians are the elected officials that influence public policy and decision making. Perhaps the best paid and least productive employees that money can buy. No other group is better than they at putting in long hours and squabbling over much ado about nothing.

Instead of representing the people, they seem to represent themselves and their own agenda. When people on one side of the aisle can't agree with people on the other side about anything, something is wrong with all of them.

They had to spend long hours putting together a piece of legislation referred to as the Civil Rights Act of 1964. After passage, it outlawed discrimination based on race, color, religion, sex, or national origin. It ended unequal application of voter registration requirements and racial segregation in schools, at the workplace, and by facilities that serve the general public.

When they did it, it was hailed a landmark. It was actually a piece of legislation to fix existing legislation that they and their predecessors had intentionally enacted to restrict the influence of Blacks, and thereby, maintain segregation and control. It was shoddy legislation created by shoddy politicians and upheld by shoddy Supreme Court justices. Worst of all, it happened in the United States of America.

It was a piece of legislation that should not have been necessary, because it granted the opportunities that Blacks should have already had. Even with the patchwork, it still falls short of accomplishing what was intended. Blacks are still discriminated against, and they are still not equal.

Now, Congress is walking down the same path again—working on legislation that allows same sex marriage. It's the same path, because same sex marriage is a knot that people should have always been able to tie themselves without having to get permission from anyone. We have enough real problems to keep congress occupied, yet they occupy themselves with something that should not be their concern or anyone else's for that matter—except for those involved.

Should a person choose to be an atheist, then so be it. Should a person be disgusted with politics and refuses to vote, but yet is willing to stand by and be taken in by a political regime that goes against his or her convictions, then so be it. Should two people of the same sex choose to marry or to be lovers, but not everyone approves, then so be it.

Most of us believe that there is a God, and therefore, we believe the words of the Holy Bible. We believe that God established that marriage is to be the union between a man and a woman. Genesis 2:24 states: "Therefore a man leaves his father and his mother and cleaves to his wife, and they become one flesh.

In Matthew 19:4-5, Jesus reaffirms the passage in Genesis: "Have you not read that he who made them from the beginning made them male and female," and said, "for this reason a man shall leave his father and mother and be joined to his wife, and the two shall become one'?"

These biblical verses are cited as being the reason why same sex marriage is a sin and should not be legalized. It has been said that there are verses in the Bible that can be cited to reinforce almost any argument. However, sometimes it seems that verses in the Bible get misinterpreted. If not misinterpreted, then twisted to verify what we want to believe.

The following verse is from the Holy Bible, Exodus 22:18: "Thou shalt not suffer a witch to live." Once upon a time, Christians took that verse very seriously. Those accused of witchcraft were tried, and if convicted, they were put to death using the most painful means of execution, e.g., burning at the stake, stoned to death, hanged by the neck.

The practice ended when so called respectful citizens were tried and condemned, and when it became obvious that innocent people were being tried and put to death. Yet, when witch hunts and witch trials were popular, they were condoned by Christians with the belief that they were fulfilling the will of God as stated in the Holy Bible. It was Christians that were trying, convicting, and executing people in the name of the Holy Father via the most painful methods possible.

Same sex relationships follow the same course as witch hunts and witchcraft in the history of Christianity. They follow the same course of human frailties as we use the Bible to justify what we think is right. Yet, we fail to see it.

The day did come when Christians—not just in Colonial America, but throughout the world—realized that what they had been doing was terribly wrong. They realized that it was wrong, even though it had been written in the Holy Bible.

Christians concluded that Genesis 2:24, and Matthew 19:4-5 did not give them the right to kill people for practicing what they called witchcraft. History is repeating itself today. We have moved on to another verse in the Holy Bible—Exodus 22:18—that tells us that love between two people of the same sex is wrong.

We take it upon ourselves to judge others, but the Bible tells us that we should not. Romans 2:1: "Therefore you are inexcusable, oh man, whoever you are who judge, for in whatever you judge another you condemn yourself; for you who judge practice the same things."

If same sex relationships are wrong, then, according to the Holy Bible, God will judge and then render the punishment should there be any. We grant that God makes no mistakes. If we believe that God made us, then He made some of us heterosexual and others homosexual by His own choosing. If He makes no mistakes, then He made what He wanted. Then, who amongst us will fashion a cross, drag it to the highest hill and nail the Holy Father to it. Who amongst us will curse Him, and then tell Him that He made a mistake, when He placed homosexual beings on earth? *For sure, it will not be I.*

If being gay or lesbian is a sin, is it a bigger sin than coveting thy neighbor's wife? The answer is no. Sin is sin and without varying degrees of significance. That being so, then why is the man that coveted his neighbor's wife any different from marriage between two men or two women. Is it different, because too many of us that take it upon ourselves to judge and condemn others are guilty of being in the wrong bed? We covet our neighbor's wife, but we don't talk about it, and we never will.

There are more sins than one can count, but we give more attention to same sex marriage and same sex lovers than to any others. Could it be that those who fight so hard to outlaw same sex relationships are afraid or unsure about their own sexuality? Are they trying to prove to themselves that they are straight—heterosexual?

In every way, the blown up overreacted to issue of same sex marriage is similar to the nonsensical Salem witch trials of Colonial Massachusetts. Burning women at the stake was the epitome of ignorance and cruelty by a supposedly civilized people—Christian people. Telling people who they can or cannot marry is getting too involved in what should be personal choices. Yet, congress had to say yay or nay to make it happen or not happen. Who knows how many millions of dollars have been invested in something that they should have just turned their backs on and walked away?

CHAPTER 7

Too Quick to Kill

Every day there are run-ins of some kind between law enforcement officers and Black people—Whites too for that matter, but too often Blacks are the target. Assuming that most police officers perform their duties without prejudice, like Black people they too have been stereotyped. The general public—mainly Black people—have come to believe that all police officers are alike.

Most Blacks believe that police officers operate by their own rules while hiding behind a badge and breaching their promise to serve and protect. Whenever an officer must surrender their badge for inappropriate conduct, the statement is made that you can't judge all law enforcement officers by the actions of a few. However, it seems that the few have become many, and the number is still increasing—an unverified observation that we all hope is wrong.

It seems that we have more corrupt law enforcement officers than we may think. Some law enforcement officials and politicians think that better on the job training is needed. It does not seem rational to think that better training will keep a police officer from shooting a person in the back—referencing Michael T. Slager, the police officer that killed Walter Scott in North Charleston, South Carolina on Tuesday, May 7, 2015.

Too many police officers are able to escape punishment after committing a crime. They are bound by the same laws that all citizens of this country must obey. Yet, they do not suffer the consequences of their illegal actions ... not even when they commit murder.

The authorities responded quickly by charging officer Slager with murder. They have been much slower to respond in other cases. When they explain things to the public, most of the time we are told that the actions taken by the police were justifiable. Sometimes for sure, their definition of justifiable seems to be whatever they can hide and sidestep with an official statement of lies.

Of late, there was the police officer killing the twelve year old Black kid in Cleveland, Ohio. A 911 caller notified the police and said that the boy had a gun, but he didn't know if it was real or not. When the police arrived on the scene, the officer claimed that he told the boy to put his hands up, but he didn't.

A video showed that the officer shot the boy in less than a minute after his arrival. That is not enough time to assess the situation and say, "Put your hands up." In order to talk to the boy and then fire a deadly shot, the officer must have been rather close. The policeman should have recognized that the suspect was just a kid, and that deadly force was unnecessary … not then.

Police officers in Florida were caught using photos of Black men for target practice. A group of national guardsmen came in afterwards and one of them recognized a photo of his brother all riddled with bullet holes. The chief of police told the news media that using the photographs was ill-considered, but no laws had been violated.

The reality is that the response from the chief of police was ill-considered and utterly despicable. He didn't see anything wrong with it, yet he is in charge of his officers. If the chief of police is too dumb to see anything wrong with using photos of Blacks for target practice, then he is too dumb to be the chief of police.

Such a response is absent of intellect, and it reflects no sensitivity or regards for Black people. If nothing was wrong, why did they not use photographs of their family members for target practice. They must have had photos of their sons and daughters, spouses, and friends. Each officer could have brought their own target with them—even a photograph of himself or herself, or a photo of the chief of police would have been appropriate.

Police officers in New York, city killed a Black man with a choke hold during an arrest. The man was suspected of selling untaxed cigarettes on the street. No gun was involved, and there were enough police officers on the scene to wrestle a twelve hundred pound steer to the ground.

Yet, what happened was considered justifiable—killing a man for selling untaxed cigarettes on the street. Excessive force was used, and it should be obvious. It's like swinging a tennis racket to swat fly that's circling around while you're eating a fish sandwich.

Black people are afraid of the police and they have reason to be. What scares them is that they don't know the good cops from the bad ones—those that are too quick to draw their weapon and fire a deadly shot. Wondering if any good cops are left is a legitimate concern if you are Black.

With so many law enforcement officers scattered across the country, there has to be many that perform their duties admirably and indiscriminately. However, there are too many rotten cops on the job for sure, and it seems that more and more are joining their ranks.

There was a time when police brutality was hidden—the victim was taken to some out of the way place—into a dark alley, or down some backwoods country road. They don't hide anymore, and they don't care who is looking at them. The scene today is like making a movie. People standing around watching—the cameras are not rolling, but iPhones are capturing the action and then it's posted on the social media.

Police officers commit crimes, yet they are not overly concerned about repercussions. They have no need to be, because they know that very seldom will anything be done about it. Should anything develop, the chief of police will explain it, unless it is so clear that lying would be ridiculously insane.

No one can deny that Black people are still treated unfairly in this country. Such a statement sounds absurd and out of line, but it is supported by a large collection of data that compares Blacks to Whites, e.g., arrest records, time served in jail, the severity of punishment, the death penalty vs a term in prison, and the list goes on.

Black people can walk into a store and one of the employees will follow them around like a shadow—keeping an eye on them to make sure that they don't steal anything. Being Black does not mean that you are a thief, but you are treated like one just because you are Black. We are always suspects, and we are tried and condemned before a crime is committed.

Some police officers will stop a car on the highway just because the driver is Black. I know because I was stopped for no apparent reason. A female police officer saw me leave a convenient store. She was parked behind my car; when I left the store, she pulled out behind me. About five miles down the highway, she stopped me. She walked up and asked to see my driver's license, registration, and proof of insurance. After looking at the documents, she said that I could go.

As she was walking away, I asked, "Why did you stop me." She said, "You don't have but one headlight." Yet, she never mentioned the headlight until I asked, and she had never been in front of my car during the encounter. I got out of the car and walked around to have a look. She walked back, stood next to me and said, "Well, it's back on now."

The headlight had never been out, and the vehicle was new. Standing there beside me was the first time that she had been in front of my car. She stopped me because I am Black—that had to be the reason, because nothing else was out of line … just the color of my skin. She lied, but I did not discuss it with her. It was almost midnight, on a dark stretch of interstate highway, and I was afraid to do much of anything other than drive away.

Being pulled over by the police officer for no legal reason was an inconvenience, but more than that, it was racial profiling. It happens thousands of times every day. A person is stopped and questioned just because they are Black.

Yet, we are always told to respect the police officers. It is hard for Blacks—or anyone else for that matter—to have respect for someone that may or may not clobber them over the head or shoot them. Most Black people will do what they are instructed to do by an officer of the law, but they do it more from fear than from respect.

Being roughhoused just because of your color is maddening. It creates an inner feeling that doesn't go away quickly, and when you come in contact with another police officer for whatever reason, it makes you suspicious and even afraid. At best, it is a poor analogy, but the respect that Blacks have for the police is a consideration close to that given a rattlesnake; give them a wide berth or risk being killed.

When all of the racially motivated turmoil was going on in Ferguson, Missouri in 2014—an unarmed Black man killed by a policeman—it created racial tension that spread across the country. Allowing that it may have been coincidental, television stations started showing movies that stir up old memories. For those that were too young to have any old memories, they were cut to the bone by what used to be when added on to what happens today.

Movies such as, The Butler, and Django Unchained were shown over and over again on television. During the same time, the movie, Selma, was released in theaters all across the country. They are good movies, but they reinforce what Black people are already angry about, being slapped around and expected to stand there and take it.

Movies do influence people. The right movie can increase racial tension and create hostile attitudes, especially if the timing is right and especially with Blacks. They see the coarseness of what was thought to be a bygone era that was filled with pain, suffering, and even killings.

Blacks get the feeling that after all these years, and after all that they have done, they are still in a place where they are not wanted, and not equal. Yet, they are expected to be nothing less than subservient and contented with being second class citizens. If Blacks are second class citizens, what in the name of hell is a killer cop? For that matter, what is a cop that stops a person on the highway just because they are Black?

It's plain and simple; there are too many corrupt police officers, and not enough is being done to put a stop to it. Those that are at the top and in charge are as liable as the officers that patrol the streets. Yet, they close their eyes or look the other way, while vigilantes exact their own decree on a people that have no voice.

Black people can't help but wonder if the too aggressive attitude of law enforcement officers in Ferguson, Missouri is typical of that in most cities across the country. Ferguson stands out by itself. The city has a population of twenty one thousand plus; the town is sixty seven percent Black; they have fifty White police officers and three Blacks. The mayor did say that they would hire more Black officers, but Blacks are not interested in being on the force. He did not explain why, but there may be a good reason for not wanting to be on the force.

The mayor of Ferguson, Missouri along with the chief of police should have been fired immediately. For a long time, both have been negligent in performing the duties of their office. They simply sat back with a que sera … attitude and let it happen.

Black people know too well the meaning of foul play and mistreatment. When their rights are continuously violated, it's easy to abandon rationale in exchange for hatred and skepticism. When they get fed up and become angry, then the question is asked, "What is wrong with Black people today?

It is a simple question to ask, and one that everybody should be able to answer correctly. The lack of justice and equal opportunity will do for starters. Too often, those in positions of authority—those that can do something to keep things on or near an even keel will sit and do nothing until all hell breaks loose. They only react then because all eyes are on them, and they have to say something that sounds right.

When things get ugly and out of control is when someone will step in front of the news media and say, "We need to create a better relationship in the community and in the workplace. We need to have more dialogue, more diversity, and a better understanding."

A better relationship, more dialogue and diversity is exactly what we need. The question is, "How many Black people will have to die before it happens?" Standing in the streets of Ferguson, Missouri or in Baltimore, Maryland with dozens of microphones and cameras stuck in front of your face—broadcasting coast to coast, and even around the world—is not the time to start talking about what needs to be done. It should have already been done and in effect.

Since nothing had been done, and it had been like that for a long time, there were no plans of doing anything. Everybody that knew about what was going on but did not sound an alarm should have been stripped of their positions and railroaded out. It was time to clean house.

The time to create a better relationship and talk about things is when things are moving along smoothly. Then is the time to keep the wheels of justice well-greased and friction to a minimum. Instead, no one thinks about doing anything until someone is dead and the town is burning like the fires of hell.

It is a fact that White police officers kill too many unarmed Blacks. Yet, that statement is about as senseless as saying, “Honey, I think we should have six children, that way, if one of them should die, we will still have five.” It sounds as though it’s alright to kill unarmed Blacks so long as you don’t kill too many—keep it within the acceptable limit.

There is no acceptable limit for murdering people. Wearing a blue uniform with a badge stuck on it is no excuse to kill. Just because a person is Black is no reason to become abusive.

Rarely should it be necessary to kill any unarmed person. Many times a suspect could be brought down or disabled by a shot in the arm or leg. Yet, very seldom does a police officer fire his weapon to wound a would be assailant.

If the officer feels threatened, he shoots to kill. If the suspect ends up wounded, it is because the officer was a poor marksman. It does not seem to matter what the age of the person is so long as he is Black—Black males do seem to be the preferred target. Sarcastic as it sounds, White police officers seem to have truly waged an all-out war on Blacks.

Blacks are the victims, and they have always been on the losing side of the battle for human rights. When looking into their faces, they appear to be angry, but maybe it's the look of despair presented to them by a lifetime of thrashings and from just being dog tired. Smiles seem to have gone away, or maybe they have forgotten how, because there's nothing much to smile about anymore.

Like Native Americans, Blacks have been promised more than they can remember. However, they do remember those promises that were kept. They stand out, because they are few, and they were hard to come by.

Whenever shady dealings are brought to light, whether it be with the police, the school system, corporate America, or anyplace else, those in charge act surprised.

Yet, Blacks are supposed to be satisfied when they promise a thorough investigation so that they can fix things and set them right.

Those in charge already know that their dealings are less than fair, but they sit quietly by and let it continue until they are exposed. That's when they act surprised and start making promises. All of the promises have been made before. Yet, this time they expect Blacks to believe that change is on the way—things are going to be better.

The president of a university or a large corporation knows from the start whether or not they have a diverse population in the workplace. Not just in the workplace, but also in positions of authority. Should they not, they usually leave it alone until there is an outcry from the public or from within.

What happened in Ferguson, Missouri and Baltimore, Maryland are prime examples of what happens when public officials shirk their responsibilities and let problems go unsolved. The big problem being an out of control police force—a police force more akin to a vigilante committee. Scars were put on Ferguson and on Baltimore that should have never been made. They are scars that will be there forever; even if they heal, there will always be reminders.

It had become obvious to local citizens that Ferguson and Baltimore had problems that must be remedied. Records showed that Blacks had been targeted by the almost all White police force in Ferguson for a long time. Deliberately one-sided as they were, it takes more than a few days to set right the things that have been wrong for so long. The biggest thing that needs fixing is restoring confidence in the minds of the public, so that they can trust and have confidence in the police.

Blacks in Ferguson and Baltimore had gotten the attention of White people from across the country. They too had recognized the ugly face of discrimination and abuse toward Blacks. Whites supported their cause, many stood with them, and more and more are siding with Blacks in their fight for human rights.

Police brutality toward Blacks goes on and on, and it will not stop until police officers are truly held accountable for their actions. Meanwhile, Blacks are viewed as being the problem—"in the streets raising hell when they should be at work. They should go home and let the authorities take care of things." Blacks are in the streets raising hell, because the authorities are not doing a damned thing other than sitting on their hands. When they are not sitting on their hands, they're crippling or killing Blacks.

Those in authority are as much to blame for the chaos going on in cities as the police officers are that keep on killing. Black people are tired of hearing the same pack of lies over and over. They are lies because nothing changes.

Even with the obvious miscarriage of justice by police officers, the looting, and the destruction of property by Blacks gets more criticism than cops committing murder. Black lives matter to Black people, but not so much to some Whites.

In spite of the police brutality that takes place, every law abiding citizen should have a place somewhere in their heart and in their mind for the good police officers.

They serve and protect and they do it admirably. As of May 12, 2015, 43 police officers had been killed in this country. They died on duty, while proudly honoring their badge and their sworn oath to serve and protect.

CHAPTER 8

THE FEDERAL GOVERNMENT

THE FEDERAL GOVERNMENT HAS PLAYED a starring role in keeping Black people chained down even after telling them that they were free back during the civil war. They were at center stage up until the mid-1960's. The Southern States were allowed to enact Black Codes—Jim Crow laws to restrict the rights of Blacks.

Poll taxes were enacted—they were legal fees that citizens had to pay before they could vote. Black people didn't have any money, and therefore, they could not vote, because they couldn't pay the fee. Voting rights were restricted even further. Should by chance someone just happened to have enough money to pay the poll tax, they had to make it past another hurdle.

To show that they were competent enough to vote, they had to pass a test. They were asked to do such things as, "recite the Preamble to the Constitution of the United States. What rights are granted to the citizens of this country by the Fifth Amendment to the United States Constitution? How do you calculate the diameter of a circle?"

Blacks did not know the answer to such questions and neither did many Whites. However, it was a Jim Crow law that served its' purpose. It was a legal means of keeping Blacks out of politics without violating any laws. The federal government didn't care, because the Supreme Court of the United States ruled that such requirements were legal.

The Supreme Court, the highest court in the land, supposedly made up of some of the best legal minds in the country, but they didn't see anything wrong with Jim Crow laws. The federal government allowed Southern

States to discriminate against Blacks for another century after the Civil War had ended. They enacted state legislation for the sole purpose of maintaining White supremacy and keeping a tight rein on Blacks.

Jim Crow laws no longer exist in federal, state, or local legislation. However, Blacks are still the victims of many of those illegal bygone yet still practiced rules and regulations that serve the same purpose today as they did more than a century ago.

Blacks are reckoned with by a justice system that knocks them down every time they stand up. They are sometimes falsely accused and then punished by a system that is far from being right. It all takes place under the guise of federal, state and local laws that promise fair and equal treatment. It is a legal system that is and always has been something less than what it claims to be. Blacks live in a country where they are not welcomed, and they may never be.

After being convicted and serving a term in prison—for something that they may or may not have done—Blacks are forever regarded as criminals and misfits by many Whites. They then become the norm to which most other Blacks are compared. Many are forced into poverty after repeatedly being denied the opportunity to be an asset rather than a burden on society. Still, society wonders what it is that keeps Blacks depressed and at the bottom.

Very seldom do people's attitudes change overnight. From the beginning, the United States was not a place for Blacks to enjoy the American way of life. They were brought here and enslaved for hundreds of years, and then they were told that they are free—but free to do what?

Hundreds of thousands of misinformed freed Blacks left the south and headed north after the Civil War ended. They had high hopes, because their minds had been reinforced with the belief that life would be better—it was the North that had liberated them from bondage. After arriving, they soon realized that attitudes do not change with longitudes.

Citizens in the North were as arrogant as those in the South. They were in a different place, but still unwanted. They were free from the legalized institution of slavery, but then they were restricted by newly enacted laws that held back more than what freedom had given.

White people had a big head start on Blacks which allowed them to get to where they are—they should be out front. Even with the head start, there are a lot of poor Whites. Although frowned upon by the White upper echelon, they are still given a better deal than poor Blacks.

It hasn't been long since the door was opened for Blacks. Even then, it wasn't flung open wide—just enough to let a few squeeze through at a time. Considering how Blacks have been forced to be at the bottom and what they have had to deal with to keep from sinking even further, is it any wonder that they are amongst the poorest in the country.

Blacks have been down so long that it seems like they are right where they belong. The attitude of some is, "why bother about crawling out just to end up right back in the same hole?" Most people will turn the other cheek a few times, but after a while, they stop and start fighting. It is a response rather similar to that of a wild animal being chased. Formidable as he is, a mighty grizzly will run to try and get away, but when he gets too tired to run anymore, he will stop and fight.

Black people today may be like the grizzly … tired of running. Yet, in the eyes and minds of many Whites, Blacks have been stereotyped, and recognized as truly being a lazy race of people. Some are, but no more so than Whites.

Most Blacks would rather have a job and earn their way. However, the jobs that are offered to Blacks are too often those that are rejected by Whites, or they are reserved for Blacks—low end with low wages. Yet, Blacks are expected to do better, but with what when they can barely eke out a living with what's made available to them.

Blacks in this country are treated just well enough to make it look like somebody cares. Politicians love a Black vote as much as they do a White vote. When the political race is on, they find their way to the Black neighborhoods—making speeches and promising to do the right things to solicit votes.

After they have been elected, they forget their way back to the people that helped put them in office. They go unremembered and unneeded until the next election. It's a cycle that is repeated in every election by every politician.

Some White people become afraid when they find themselves in a crowd of mostly Black people. In spite of what they may have heard or seen, most Blacks are not violent. They would rather laugh and talk than fuss and fight. Most Blacks are out and about for the same reasons as Whites … taking care of business and not looking for trouble.

It will be a long time—and the day may never come—when White and Black people will both offer the other an olive branch and reconcile their differences. Yet, it is something that we could do if we would let the past get lost somewhere in the back of our minds.

We have become too satisfied with the way things have always been, and we are unwilling to change. Instead of settling for what we are, we should dare ourselves to bury the hatchet, but only after we've severed a branch from an olive tree.

Undoubtedly, there are some, but not a lot of White politicians in Washington care very much about Blacks.

For that matter, it seems that very few politicians care much about anything other than themselves. Whenever something good comes out of Washington that benefits Blacks, it is usually fallout from something intended for another purpose.

The attitudes of both White and Black people in the United States changed with the election of Barack Obama. Poor Blacks had the expectation that they would be the focal point of the new president's agenda. They thought that their long awaited for ship had finally arrived. Some didn't know that it is impossible for a Black president to put money into their pockets.

Many White people regretted that the United States had elected a Black man as president. The majority of Whites never have wanted a Black president just because they had never had one. Aside from that, it's a job for White people.

Republicans in congress changed with the election of President Obama. In the past, the two parties—Democrats and Republicans—had been able to compromise when necessary, but not with a Black president. The Republicans have stood in front of everything that Democrats have tried to do.

Republicans blamed things that went wrong during the administration of George Bush on Barack Obama. President Bill Clinton left a surplus budget when his last term in office ended. That surplus was squandered by the Republicans under the leadership of George Bush. However, today's deficit is blamed on President Obama.

We should not expect the financial and social problems in this country to be resolved until we have a congress that is color blind. They let the clock tick down almost to the final hour before passing legislation that would keep the government operating. Once, they even let it expire, closing down national parks and barring tourists from visiting landmarks in Washington, D.C. they did it because the United States of America has a Black president, and that is not a good reason.

The Republican Party caters to White America. The Democrat Party caters to America, regardless of color or ethnic heritage. Without the support of White voters, Barack Obama would have never been elected. Mitt

Romney may have won the election had the Republican Party paid more attention to minorities.

The Republican Party must learn to woo and court the diverse population of this country. Presidential elections can no longer be won when relying mainly on White voters. People have changed, but the Republican Party has not evolved in years. They are still holding on to yesteryear—living and thinking in the past.

CHAPTER 9

POVERTY AND RACISM

POVERTY IS CLOSELY ASSOCIATED WITH racism. Since the two are tied together, public sentiments and practices associated with being poor lead to more racism. In addition to racism, poverty has three other close companions, lack of education, inadequate housing, and lack of adequate health care. As a result, poverty is passed from one generation to the next and it affects minorities the most.

Social status can change the way we see a person's race, according to Dr. Aliya Saperstein, Assistant Professor of Sociology, University of California, Berkeley. The simple process of moving from the inner city to the suburbs can change our perception of people. "Race is not just an ascribed-at-birth, fixed characteristic," Saperstein said. Instead, "race implies a set of gendered expectations for behavior against which people are continually judged. In short, there is a direct relationship between racial accord and socioeconomic status."

Education would no doubt rid the world of a lot of racism, but if education means everybody going to college, it will not happen. Education as a tool to combat racism is something that we can teach ourselves and it's not complicated. It starts with replacing the frown on our face with a smile when we meet someone. Instead of looking the other way, look at each other and speak. In this case, education is just a matter of knowing right from wrong, having respect for others, and learning to understand the diverse cultures around us.

We must learn to communicate with each other effectively—both verbally and with gestures—it's that simple. We know that racial hatred is wrong without ever walking onto a college campus. It does not take a lot of effort to educate ourselves and earn high marks in treating people right.

People in the upper crust—both Black and White—tend to socialize together more often than those at the other end of the spectrum. If they are around each other enough, they usually become well acquainted and spend a lot of time talking. They get to know each other personally.

One of the biggest barriers that keep us separated is the lack of communication—never getting to know what the other is like. Yet, it's so easy to do if we would only let ourselves do it. Instead of doing it, we continue segregating ourselves while intentionally practicing a social lifestyle that our forefathers fought and died for us to have.

One can look around and see that social position does change our perceptions of race—how we see and feel about people whose color is different from ours. Whites are likely to be more friendly toward minorities when their socioeconomic status is equal to theirs. Eliminating poverty would surely increase social status, but views differ widely on whether or not poverty will ever be eliminated or if it's even possible.

Dr. Jim Yong Kim, President of the World Bank Group stated that the World Bank has a goal of ending extreme poverty by the year 2030 and boosting prosperity. (October 7, 2013, UN News Center)

He explained that the best way to lift a person out of extreme poverty is with a good job. In order to do that, economies have to grow. Economic growth hinges on the countries of the world developing improved policy, improving business environments and attracting investors. He explained further that it has to be done in such a manner that growth occurs even in the poorest of countries, including the private sector. The plan must be all inclusive—including everyone—thereby creating stability, because people are not going to continue accepting being poor according to Dr. Kim.

Bill Gates, American business magnate and philanthropist has a vision similar to that of Dr. Jim Yong Kim.

Gates says that poverty should be almost eliminated by the year 2035. Although criticized, he notes that aid to the poor is effective, but it can be made more effective so that it eliminates some of the waste. He further states that wealthy countries need to make policy changes that open up their markets and cut agricultural subsidies, while poor countries need to spend more on health and development for their own people.

As always, at the other end of the spectrum are those that believe that poverty is here to stay. It is a label stuck on some, because they don't have as much when compared to others. In other words, if the gap separating the groups is too wide, then the group at the lower end is poor. Hence the phrase, "as the rich get richer, the poor get poorer," because the gap widens.

Today, any poor person would be on easy street and set for life if someone would give them one million dollars. However, if suddenly everybody else has a billion dollars, the person with one million dollars is again poor. He is poor, because of the huge gap that separates his worth from that of others.

One must take into account the fact that if rising above poverty depends on a person's willingness to scratch and claw their way up, then what. It is a factor to consider, because a lot of people are afraid that they may break out in a sweat if they have to put forth too much effort. Not everyone wants to work hard to achieve more.

There are a lot of people that would rather sit back and take whatever life has thrown at them and be satisfied. They don't mind being lazy and jobless as long as their lifestyle is subsidized. Consequently, they are satisfied with things just the way they are.

When you look around at those that have limited income, they seem to be far less frugal with what they have than those that are more fortunate. Any person that is able bodied, yet they find themselves in the lazy category, jobless and of course poor, then so be it. There's nothing that anyone can do or say to them that will generate the desire to become an asset to society rather than a burden. Since they are satisfied with hanging on by a thread, leave them alone and let them dangle. They are what they are by choice.

President Lyndon B. Johnson declared war on poverty in 1964 when the poverty rate in this country was close to twenty percent. Today the poverty rate is down almost twenty five percent compared to what it was then—a significant difference, but it took fifty years. During those fifty years, relationships between Black people and White people have improved tremendously. Yet, the fact remains; we still have a lot of racial problems in the United States of America and throughout the world.

Some Whites don't care whether or not poverty is eliminated. Their opinion is that Blacks are right where they need to be. If they are poor, then let them be poor. They have the same opinion of poor Whites, and they regard them as society's trash.

Black people use the phrase, "the man is out to get us," the man being the White race of people. Race related problems are going to be around for a long time. Since sociologists believe that eliminating poverty improves race relations, the process of eliminating poverty could be accelerated if it was something that "the man" really wanted to do? However, it would mean laying aside moral values and taking on the mindset of a maniac.

In the effort to combat poverty, should the man decide to lay waste to all poor Blacks, there would be a huge decrease in poverty. While they are at it, there would be no need to stop there. They could go ahead and rid the country of both poor Blacks and Whites, and thereby eliminate poverty completely. It would rid the country of all expenditures associated with helping the poor, and ease the burden on the working class. The United States would soon be debt free.

Laying waste to all poor people could not be a process of genocide; that would make the country look too much like Nazi Germany under the rule of Adolph Hitler. It would have to be a process that would not arouse too much suspicion of wrongdoing. Even when someone figures out that things aren't right, it would have to be something that could be explained with a bunch of lies and still sound believable.

To avoid creating an alarm and a lot of suspicion, the cleanup would have to take place over a long period of time. An effective, low keyed operation could go on for years without arousing concern. Vital statistics could easily be falsified to facilitate the operation.

Human sterilization would get the job done. Both men and women would become infertile, and therefore, incapable of reproduction. The near perfect as possible causal agent could be added to the food supply that the government provides to the needy. Quality and quantity of food could both be increased. Employing such a tactic would even reassure people's faith in their government.

The process could go on for a long period of time without being noticed. Some non-targeted segments of the population—well to-do Whites and Blacks—would be affected. However, such a mishap would be tolerated, and it would add credence to the lies being told to explain things to the people.

The increased rate of sterility would not appear to be related to race or gender, and they would have the fraudulent vital statistics to back it up. The reports would show that whatever is happening is widespread and it affects the entire population. If well managed, such an underhanded clandestine operation could go on indefinitely without causing a panic.

When the process is over, the number of poor in the country would be reduced dramatically. With such a mass of people, there is always a few that would escape the plan. However, they could easily be taken care of or they could be left alone to continue life as usual.

Should the survivors ever be able to figure out what had taken place—or have an inkling of what might have happened—anyone that is poor or getting close to being poor would probably be willing to work like a horse to stay above the poverty line.

The United States would be in the Black—the national debt that is—and it would serve as a model for other countries of the world. They too would surely follow the same path. Should such a devious undertaking ever take place, other countries would find out about it, because nothing can be kept hidden anymore—not forever. For that matter, foreign countries could even be in on it, and make it a worldwide joint operation.

Absurd as it sounds, it is possible to do. Consequently, the man may not be your friend, but he is not out to get you—not as much as you may think. In a country with forty five million Blacks and two hundred and seventy one million non-Blacks—they could wipe out the entire Black race at any time. Black people wouldn't stand a chance.

Being poor is not a crime, but those living in poverty are regarded as substandard citizens whether they be White or Black. They depend on various social programs in order to survive. Even then, life for most is miserable.

People in the United States wonder why so many billions of dollars are given to other countries rather than using it to make things better at home. The United States gives money to third world countries and to other countries that are of strategic importance. Millions of dollars are also given to other countries that are something less than friendly toward this country.

The big financial giveaways are orchestrated by our elected officials in Washington, D.C. If the money is given for strategic purposes, why not use the money within the confines of the United States. It could be used to develop strategies here at home for dealing with the rest of the world while becoming independent and strong enough to protect our own interests. The United States could stop trying to police the world.

The foreign giveaways could go into rebuilding America; it would create jobs and get people off of welfare programs. It could be used to fund research on alternative energy sources to make us less dependent on foreign oil. Energy independence or energy self-sufficient is a must do anyway, because regardless of how much oil is left underground, it will not last forever.

The United States could become self-sufficient in energy, create a strong defense system to deter any thoughts of being invaded, and get out of bed with other countries, because we owe them money. Poverty in our part of the world, and dependency on countries in other parts of the world would disappear if we first take care of ourselves.

Most African Americans, about ninety percent, support the Democrat Party. Most believe that the Republican Party is too conservative and anti-Black. Conversely, Republicans believe that the Democrats are too liberal. As a result, the two parties separate themselves like oil in water.

Race relations are strained by comments made by television and radio personalities. On July 24, 2013, Bill O'Reilly made an appearance on Geraldo Rivera's radio show. O'Reilly made the statement that many White people are afraid of Black people—young Black men in particular. O'Reilly used the George Zimmerman/Trayvon Martin case that happened in 2012 to reinforce his point. He said that Zimmerman was afraid of Martin because of the way Martin was dressed, he didn't know who he was, he became suspicious, and things got out of control.

In the case of George Zimmerman and Trayvon Martin, we only have Zimmerman's version of what happened, because he killed Martin. If Zimmerman was afraid of Martin, then he should have followed the advice of the 911 dispatcher and stayed in his car. Instead, he chose to follow Martin.

In all likelihood, the death of Martin would have been avoided if Zimmerman had done what he had been instructed to do and if he had used reason and logic. Zimmerman couldn't have been afraid. Had he been, he could have easily backed away, but he chose not to.

If Bill O'Reilly is right, "White people are afraid of Black people," it can't be used as an excuse for Whites to shoot Blacks—not even in the George Zimmerman/ Travon Martin incident. Hopefully, that is not what O'Reilly meant, but making such a statement doesn't do anything to help fix the White/Black problems that we have. It only makes them worse. Many people will listen to what O'Reilly said and interpret Zimmerman's actions as being justified—he was Black and looked suspicious—I shot him to protect myself.

Supposedly, Martin looked suspicious because of the way he was dressed. The hoodie always attracts attention.

Like it or not, people should be able to wear whatever type of clothing they wish. If the hoodie is illegal, then congress should enact another dumb law so that the public will know what to buy and what not to buy when they go shopping. Until then, when you see a person wearing one, should you become afraid, then scream like hell and run in the opposite direction.

White people have no more reason to be afraid of Black people than Black people have to be afraid of White people. *I'm Black, but White people don't scare me. When I walk down the streets, I don't see White people crossing over to the other side, because they are afraid. If we don't know each other, we usually speak and keep on walking—neither of us looking back to see if it's time to strike a trot.*

On the O'Reilly Factor, October 30, 2014, O'Reilly talked with PBS radio host Travis Smiley. O'Reilly said that Republicans are afraid of Black people—a comment very similar to the one he had made earlier on Geraldo Rivera's radio show. When Smiley asked why, O'Reilly said that the White Republican power is afraid of Black Americans. He explained why by saying that they are afraid because White Republicans don't know how to treat them so they just stay away. That's one hell of a way to solve a problem.

Assuming that O'Reilly is correct in his assessment, then it seems that Republicans should start doing something to catch up. They should start listening and talking to the people that they don't understand. The Republican Party makes decisions every day that affects the Black people of this country. They cannot adequately and justly represent a people that they do not know.

If White Republicans truly do not understand Black people, then being afraid is a legitimate concern. Yet, White Republicans have been looking at Black people since the Republican Party was founded in 1854—looking but unable to see. From then until now is long enough to figure something out even by trial and error, but apparently they haven't tried at all.

As a Black person, I know as much about White people as White people know about themselves. I know their needs, their feelings, their desires and their pains. The biggest difference between us is nothing more than the color of our skin.

Republicans should know the same thing about Black people, because our needs are no different from theirs. The color of a person's skin is nothing more than the color of their skin. The things that make them tick are the same … no more and no less.

African Americans have been in this country for about four hundred years—starting as farm laborers, domestics, carpenters, mill workers, etc., and finally to the office of President of the United States—but you don't know us. Do you not know us, or do you prefer not to know us?

Saying that "you don't know us" is ridiculous, but it may well be true. It is apparent that Bill O'Reilly is not the only White person that does not know us. Former mayor of New York City, Rudolph Giuliani said that President Obama does not love America.

Giuliani would have been right on target had he expanded his remarks and said, "Black people do not love America as much as White people." It would have definitely been a true statement. Yet, he would not understand the reason why.

Whites in this country have had a long courtship with America, one that has been quite fruitful. Blacks, on the other hand have had something more akin to a one night stand. Blacks are still licking the wounds that have been inflicted and not yet healed—wounds caused not by the lash, but by a government of the people that has never cared much about people of color.

It has not been long since Blacks were slaves, it has not been long since they were lynched, it has not been long since they were allowed to vote, and it has not been long since they were allowed to enter through the front door. Fall in love with her—someday maybe, but not yet.

In spite of having a relationship that does not overflow with love, America is still our home and our country of choice, because life here is better than any place else that we know. If necessary, we will stand and fight to defend her to the end—many of us have done so—Whites should not criticize Blacks because their affections for America are not as deep as theirs.

Blacks may not love America as much as Whites, but Blacks love America more than America love's Blacks.

America was satisfied with Blacks being here when they were slaves and stuck in the cotton fields. When slavery was abolished, Blacks became the stepchild of a sick money making system that had died. Since then, they have been lynched, denied their civil rights, and then criticized as being everything that is less than good.

Some of us have a problem interpreting numbers. Then there are some that don't have a problem, yet they manipulate the numbers to reflect what they want them to show. Some reports show that there are more White people on welfare in the United States than there are Blacks.

When considering the entire population of people, there are more Whites on welfare than there are Blacks. The reason is that there are more White people in this country than there are Blacks. Therefore, the numbers are correct, but it's like comparing apples to oranges.

When comparing apples to apples and oranges to oranges, the numbers get flip flopped. When comparing the percentage of poor Whites to the entire population of Whites, and then the percentage of poor Blacks compared to the entire population of Blacks, the numbers are more meaningful. In this case, likes are compared to likes. Not only is it more meaningful, it is the correct way to make the comparison. Each race is compared to itself rather than across races.

Being referred to as a burden on society is a constant criticism about Blacks, since the percentage of Blacks on welfare is higher than the percentage of Whites—about twenty seven percent vs ten percent. There is a huge difference, but there are logical reasons due to mitigating circumstances that account in part for the disparity.

Admittedly, among both races there are some that do not want a job other than the one they already have which is doing nothing. Yet, there are others that don't have a job simply because they are Black—White employees are preferred over Blacks.

When business is such that some employees must be dismissed or laid off, that is when Blacks get preferential treatment. Only then are they moved to the front of the line. It is true that Blacks are the last to be hired and the first to be fired—in this example, laid off. As a result, they stay at the bottom of the heap.

CHAPTER 10

POPULATION AND CHANGE

THERE IS A LIMIT ON the earth's capacity to supply resources necessary to sustain life. As usual, scientists cannot agree on how many people earth can support, but the number being tossed around suggest about ten billion. In 1798 English scholar, Thomas Malthus, submitted that the population of human beings increases faster than the earth's capacity to produce resources necessary for survival. He theorized the following:

> *The power of population is so superior to the power of the earth to produce subsistence for man, that premature*

death must in some shape or other visit the human race. The vices of mankind are active and able ministers of depopulation. They are the precursors in the great army of destruction, and often finish the dreadful work themselves. But should they fail in this war of extermination, sickly seasons, epidemics, pestilence, and plague advance in terrific array, and sweep off their thousands and tens of thousands. Should success be still incomplete, gigantic inevitable famine stalks in the rear, and with one mighty blow levels the population with the food of the world." (Malthus 1798. An Essay on the Principle of Population)

Scientists believe that planet earth can sustain a population of ten billion people, but not as we are today. Eating habits would have to change by consuming more vegetable crops and less meat. An acre of farmland will produce far more edible food in the form of grains, fruits and vegetables than when fed to livestock that are then slaughtered for human consumption.

The time could come when if prime cuts of meat are available, they will be only for the wealthy—the price will be too high for the working class. What used to be tossed in the garbage will be kept and consumed later. Then, leftovers from the day before will taste better than they do today.

The highways are still filled with gas guzzlers, but they don't drink as much as they once did. Things staying the way they are, the world's petroleum reserves will someday be depleted. Not depleted to the point that less thirsty cars will solve the problem, but depleted to the point that none will be available. However, advancements in science and technology will replace petroleum with some other form of renewable energy. Still, the horse and buggy are probably gone for good.

Society changes with the population of people. Small increases result in changes that are so subtle that they are hardly noticeable. When the population gets so high that it puts a strain on society, things will have already changed dramatically. People become more concerned about their own livelihood and less concerned about that of others.

Today, death and dying are troublesome, but not so much as in an overpopulated world. When supplies get to be in short supply and long term, the value of a human life decreases. The human instinct for survival becomes more like that of an animal—attention shifts more toward one's self and less toward others, even family. So much so that we get to the point where death no longer matters—or at least, not nearly as much as it once did.

Overpopulation and the impact that it will have on mankind is something that most of us never think about. If we do, we simply say, "It's so far into the future that it will not affect me." However, we should not want it to affect our children or our children's children.

Earth will be drastically changed. If not by some catastrophic event, or a series of catastrophic events, e.g., earthquakes, floods, famine, diseases, or wars that will thin the ever increasing population of people, then by the people themselves. If left unchecked, it will happen sometime within the next one hundred years. Should it happen, it will be a catastrophe unequaled in the history of mankind.

Currently, the world produces enough food so that no one should go hungry. However, thousands upon thousands of people die from malnutrition every year. In addition to hunger, thousands upon thousands die every year from diseases resulting from the lack of adequate health care. They are the poor souls that we in the industrialized world do not care about and have chosen to ignore.

Hunger and disease are two of the most effective means of purposefully eliminating or thinning a population of people without sounding an alarm. Thousands of people die every day in undeveloped third world countries because of malnutrition and the lack of adequate health care.

In a hungry world, everybody becomes an aggressive hunter. Wild animals such as deer, rabbits, squirrels, game birds, fish and the like would be the first to disappear. Then, attention would turn to animals that have never been widely considered as a source of food for human consumption. When the masses get hungry, almost anything becomes food.

It would be next to impossible for farmers and ranchers to grow crops and raise animals for slaughter to meet the demands of the general public. The fruits of their labors would be stolen and consumed by the hungry before reaching the marketplace. Growing a garden and the freezing and canning of food at home would not be of much advantage. It would only be an invitation for the hungry to break in and strip the cupboard bare.

The lack of food rids the mind of love and compassion and enhances the instinct of sole survival. Extreme hunger can even create a population of human cannibals. It would again become a world of, "survival of the fittest."

In the absence of sufficient and effective mechanisms of population control, mankind could possibly revert back to the days of yore. It could become a world where humans would be on the order of scavengers with a mentality akin to that of savages. Hunger hurts and the hungry will go to unbelievable extremes in order to stay alive. When the essentials for human survival become limited, then the haves become the prey of the have-nots.

Emma Lazarus' words scribed on the pedestal of the Statute of Liberty, "give me your tired, your poor, your huddled masses yearning to breathe free, … ." have lost their meaning.

Illegal immigrants enter the United States every day—mainly via the southern border—but they are not welcomed with open arms. In fact, they are unwanted. Furthermore, the influx of people into this country from foreign lands will increase due to hunger, diseases, and crippling catastrophic events in other parts of the world. If the masses must leave their native lands, the United States of America will be their place of choice to seek refuge and citizenship.

They will come here, because this is the country that they have been told about, the country that welcomes outsiders and offers equal opportunity for all. They have heard of her shortcomings, but they refuse to believe that America is anything other than paradise.

Still, all will not settle in this country. They will settle across the globe, but in places that are not considered third world. Rather, their new lands will be the industrialized countries where living accommodations are more accommodating than their homelands. They will seek refuge in places where food is more plentiful and where medical facilities are available to treat the sick. Almost any place would be better than what they will have left behind.

The forced exodus from third world countries will give birth to a huge increase in the population of all industrialized nations. Living conditions and attitudes will be strained, because people will be forced closer together. Then, whatever the face of racism was like in the past will become uglier than ever before.

CHAPTER 11

Human Guinea Pigs

Scientists speculate that the Ebola virus outbreak in West Africa may have come from just one person that was infected by a bat and then spread to other people. Likewise, one can also speculate that a single person was intentionally infected with the virus—perhaps knowingly or unknowingly—and then it spread to other people. That the infection was a deceptively intentional act bears as much credence as being infected by a bat. Since no one knows for sure, one guess is as good as the other.

Blacks in Africa have been dying from hunger and disease for a long time. Who's to say that the process is not given a boost from time to time to speed things along? It would be an easy thing to do, and it would not require a lot of manpower to get it done if the avenue was via the introduction of more diseases.

The introduction of more diseases to go along with those that they already have would not arouse much attention. Such a low-key tactic would augment the already high death rate caused by disease and starvation. No one would be able to point a finger at anyone, because everything would appear to be normal.

Admittedly, such a thought sounds heinous, but it's not unthinkable when considering the atrocities that take place every day—barbaric acts that are gut-wrenching to the point that a person has to eat dinner before listening to the evening news. Otherwise, risk the loss of appetite or the urge to vomit during the course of dining.

Gaining access to deadly biological agents is far from being impossible. The Centers for Disease Control receives several reports every year of lost bioterror germs and toxins. Therefore, it seems apparent that a person could easily smuggle out a small quantity of a deadly contagious agent and pass it on to someone else. That person could transport the material to wherever and expose a single person or multiple individuals. While speculating, who can say with certainty that such an underhanded occurrence has not already taken place?

Since deadly biological agents getting lost from inventory is not uncommon, who's to say that the Ebola outbreak in Africa was not born from such a callous scheme. It's doubtful that anyone knows when the first sample of any biological agent was lost from inventory. That being the case, it's possible that tens of thousands of people may have already died as a result of being purposefully infected by the introduction of man-made infectious pathogens.

The Ebola outbreak in West Africa became a global issue only after two American health care workers were infected and returned to the United States. According to Laura Seay, Assistant Professor at Colby College, Waterville, Maine, they were secretly treated with an experimental serum at a clinic while still in Monrovia, the capital of Liberia.

One of the two Americans that were treated was a physician. Realizing that they had no other options, the two Americans willingly took the experimental serum. After being treated, they were then transported to Emory Hospital in Atlanta, Georgia and on the road to recovery.

When the public was informed of the successful treatment of the two Americans, it created excitement with hopes and expectations of medical relief for Blacks in West Africa. Shortly afterwards, hopes and expectations were replaced with somber cries of disregard for Black people as care had been afforded the privileged White race. People began to wonder why the Black person that worked at the clinic and contracted Ebola did not receive the same treatment as the White workers.

The process of events was viewed by some as unethical and race related. Those that had accused pharmaceutical companies of using Blacks as guinea pigs were reprimanded. Whites had become the guinea pigs since they were the first to receive the experimental Ebola serum. Yet, the question has merit. "Were they really guinea pigs?"

Ebola is a deadly virus. When a person knows that they have been infected by any deadly agent of which there is no known cure, they will quickly volunteer to be a guinea pig. Knowing that the experimental drug may be deadly itself, at least they feel that there is a chance of surviving.

The two Americans volunteering to be guinea pigs and consenting to be treated with a serum that may or may not save their lives is completely different from saying that Africans are used as guinea pigs. The difference is that the two Americans understood what they were doing and they knew the consequences of not consenting to treatment.

The rest of the world does not care much about what happens to Black people in Africa so long as what happens in Africa stays in Africa. If they did, more would be done to alleviate the pain and suffering. Instead, the plan seems to be aimed at eliminating Blacks by letting them die from hunger and diseases. If not that, then let them be the test subjects to advance technology for the privileged.

Africans and African Americans have been used as guinea pigs since their first encounter with White Europeans, and they still are today. White America will argue the point, but Blacks have been lied to for so long that they are now skeptical of almost any words that come from Whites.

It is a fact that Black Africans are guinea pigs for chemical companies. Companies go to Africa to test pharmaceutical products and other biological agents that might be used as weapons for biological warfare. They can conduct studies on humans without a lot of red tape and with little or no opposition. The nature of their testing is kept secret and only a few are privy to what is going on.

Today, Africa is a breeding ground for diseases and sickness like no other place on the planet. It's always attributed to malnutrition and unsanitary conditions. It is not unlikely that much of it is due to unethical testing by giant corporations whose first goal is to make money at almost any cost.

Should there be any mishaps or should anything go awry, they are prepared to deal with it when it happens. A pharmaceutical company can sometimes get away with it. Pfizer, Inc. did not. It is the perfect laboratory to conduct efficacy studies and to determine side effects which are prerequisites to registration and marketing. The case against Pfizer is just one, but it serves to reinforce the statement that, "not many care about what happens in Africa."

Pfizer was testing a new antibiotic, trovafloxacin (Trovan), to determine efficacy and possible side effects when used to treat meningitis. Had the test results been positive, it would have been a major medical breakthrough. Even then, it would have been the wrong thing to do, because it was an amoral act of science conducted on an unknowing people for corporate gain.

A lawsuit was filed against Pfizer and they chose to settle out of court to the tune of seventy five million dollars. Settling out of court is right next to an admission of guilt. Pfizer's lack of ethics did not generate a lot of public attention, because those that were treated and died along with those that were treated but managed to survive were all Africans.

CHAPTER 12

MAINTAING THE WHITE MAJORITY

~

THE UNITED STATES OF AMERICA without a White majority—what would it be like—would it be better or worse? One would think that the country would be better when we are all mixed to the point that we can no longer discriminate or be prejudiced toward the other based on race. Yet, there has been other ethnic groups in world history—Africans, Native Americans, Europeans, etc.—that fought amongst themselves, yet they shared a common heritage. They had been separated by their inability to resolve differences within their own culture. When they couldn't, then they fought for years on end.

It is not unthinkable that the same thing could happen again in this country. Chaotic and messed up as it is, it is possible that we could be experiencing the most peaceful years since the birth of this nation.

The White majority has been at the center of the power structure in this country since shortly after the arrival of the first Europeans. Obviously, they want to maintain that position. They want to stay at the top, because when you've been number one long enough, it feels like there is where you belong, and it does have its' perks—in particular, less discrimination and you get to call the shots.

Many of us will be in our graves and not see it happen, but it has already started taking place. Should things keep going the way they are, the day will come when you will not have to put a check mark in that little box that identifies your race. Eventually, the peoples of this country will all be mixed to the point that skin color will be meaningless.

What used to be Black and White and whatever else will become a mixture of all. You will have two choices, you can like it if you want to, or you can hate it. Nobody really cares which choice you make, and there's nothing short of genocide that you can do to stop it. Therefore, get used to it and live with it, or dislike it and be miserable.

By the year 2042, racial minority groups will make up the majority of the population in the United States according to the United States Census Bureau. The Pew Research Center is a nonpartisan American think tank based in Washington, D.C. They provide information on social issues, public opinion, and demographic trends shaping the United States and the world.

They released the results of a study examining generations and the country's changing demographics. Their study shows that the population of White Americans in the United States will decrease from the current 85% to 43% percent by the year 2060. Whites will constitute 43% of the total population by the year 2060, but it is predicted that they will no longer be the majority by the year 2043.

The predicted change is due to an increase in immigration and a higher birth rate of minorities. The population of non-Whites in this country is growing faster than the population of Whites. The number of non-White children already make up about half the population of children under five years of age.

What will the United States of America be like when White people are no longer the majority? If they don't do something to prevent it, it will definitely happen. Should steps be taken to preserve and maintain the White majority, it will add another dark chapter to this country's already blemished past.

America faltered seriously and shamelessly with the enslavement of Blacks. She faltered by denying equal rights and opportunities to Blacks after slavery had been abolished. She faltered when women were hanged and sometimes burned at the stake as witches. With several strikes already against her, will she falter again, or will she be the pillar of justice that she claims to be?

Any actions taken for the purpose of maintaining White supremacy would be in overt defiance of human rights and the principals of democracy. However, who amongst us will deny that some will not say, "Democracy be damned," and forge ahead with the amoral objective of maintaining White supremacy. It would be that important to some.

The only question would be, "how many would join in." The force would have to be formidable enough to enter a second civil war. The war would have White supremacy advocates on one side and Whites fighting along beside Blacks on the other side. Blacks and White non-supremacists would outnumber the White supremacists.

A large number of Whites—very likely the majority—would fight alongside Blacks simply because it would be the right thing to do. They would do it because they are not bogged down with hatred, and they would want to preserve the diverse culture of America. She has always been the world's melting pot, and their wish is that she maintain her identity.

However, another civil war will not take place to maintain White supremacy. Since they would be outnumbered,

White supremacists would hold off with their plan. They would wait for another opportunity.

Should the natural course of events be allowed to continue, in thirty years or so, the shoe will be on the other foot. Mixed races of people will constitute the great majority in positions of authority. Both sides of the aisle on Capitol Hill will look like a blend of chocolate and vanilla ice cream.

White people will be the new minority. Therefore, the Congressional Black Caucus will have had its' day, but it will be replaced by the Congressional White Caucus. There will be no need for the National Association for the Advancement of Colored People; it will be replaced by the National Association for the Advancement of White People—organizational names will surely change, but for certain, they will include the word, White.

White people would have the right to identify their organizations by referencing color. They would also have the right to exclude citizens from any and all other races from becoming members. They would have the right, because Blacks did the same thing when they were the minority.

The bylaws of the Black Caucus do not mention race as a prerequisite to becoming a member. However, no non-Blacks have ever been a member. Consequently, White organizations will follow the same format.

The new regime composed of mixed races will undoubtedly be racist. Their political decisions will be biased—at least to some extent like it has always been with a majority—but then it will be flip flopped. White people will probably complain about racial profiling, police brutality, being treated as second class citizens, etc. There will be discrimination in the workplace, i.e., the best and highest paying jobs going to those of color.

Just imagine today's social problems being reversed when it comes to race. That will be the only thing different. The White race will become number two.

White people in the United States—those that could afford to do so—would probably migrate back to Europe in order to circumvent being the minority in a society that is governed by people of color. They would do so, because they have always been at the top and in charge. Having to cede their position of prominence in society, and more or less be forced to accept one of lesser standing would be too much change and too demeaning.

Migrating back to Europe could create the opportunity of a lifetime for White people. It would probably be relatively easy for them to create an alliance with groups such as al-Qaeda or ISIS and even get the backing of one or more oil rich countries. In time, they could create a rather formidable European powerhouse—especially if Russia joined in—and certainly, North Korea would want a slice of the pie.

United as one, it is possible that they could build up a military power strong enough to deter intervention by any other country or countries that might join forces with the United States. Canada would certainly be an ally of the United States. Mexico would be caught between the proverbial rock and a hard place. Unable to offer much in the form of military might, the United States and Canada would probably be satisfied with excluding her from the pact.

Realizing that they have become the supreme power, a rogue coalition would probably move ahead with a plan to clean up North America—get rid of them once and for all. The United States and Canada would not be able to stop them. They would have the option of severely crippling or total annihilation.

Should that rogue coalition carry out such a plan, North America would lay in ruins when it ended—requiring lots of backbreaking hand labor to clean up and get things back to where they should be … ruled by the White majority. With broken spirits and no will to further resist, people of color would once again be placed in bondage along with most of the Whites that had sided with them. One of the dark chapters in America's history would repeat itself. This time, however, those in chains would include both Blacks and Whites.

Having a second chance to be in the position of lord and master, White people would not make the same mistake again. They would rule with absolute authority and zero tolerance for disobedience. History will have taught them how to tend their subjects. They would know where they failed the first time, and they would get it right the next time.

The enslaved would be unable to buy their freedom, and any White sympathizers would be quickly tried and then put to death for treason. A trial would be nothing more than a scare tactic for law abiding citizens. The publicity and public execution that follows would make any would be traitors in society think twice before thinking about siding with Blacks.

Everyone would know the fate of the accused the moment they are charged. A trial would not last long—each side would have a few minutes to present their case—and a guilty verdict would not always require a preponderance of the evidence. A trial might start at nine o'clock in the morning and be over in time for lunch.

With no court of appeals, the convicted would be shot within minutes after hearing the verdict. They would get rid of him or her right away so that they wouldn't have to spend money on food and other accommodations. Law and order would certainly prevail. The shortcomings of society would be the long arm of the law and the brutal administration of justice.

White supremacy would once again rule. Yet, the big question would be, "Who would the United States of America eventually belong to?" It is very doubtful that the coalition would just give her back to the White people that originally owned her—not after all of the expenses that they will have incurred. The issue would probably be resolved with another war. It would be a war between the different factions of the rogue coalition.

The entire scenario has the ring of being outside the realm of possibilities, but wars have been fought with much less to gain. Although farfetched, it is possible that it could happen. Someone or some radical group has probably already entertained the thought.

Considering past and current immigration and social trends, it appears imminent … the White majority is on the way out; but maybe not. White people see it coming and you can be sure that they have not been sitting idly by waiting for it to happen. Consequently, there is a more civilized way of assuring that the White majority lives on.

The White majority has been holding onto an ace—not wanting to use it unless they have to—but the time has come to lay it on the table. During the 19th and 20th centuries, Asian—Chinese in particular—immigrated to the United States in large numbers and found jobs. They helped build railroads, worked in the mining industry, worked as cooks and domestics. They were willing to accept jobs that others in this country simply refused to do.

They worked hard under adverse conditions with little or no respect. They were paid less than the White employees that worked alongside them—like today in a way. They were referred to as chinks, they were hounded and abused, and not even allowed to live in some towns.

When Asian first arrived in this country, their social position was similar to that of Blacks. The difference between them being that Blacks were slaves and Asian were not. Today, Whites in America regard Asians as a highly intelligent race of people, and they along with Latinos, and Hispanics will probably be the new recruits that enable the White race to remain the White majority.

After more than one and a half centuries, the White race is willing to reach out to Asian, Latinos, and Hispanics and welcome them into their culture. The former fair skinned ethnic minorities will be counted as White in order to maintain the White majority. The process has already been set into motion.

Asians, Latinos, and Hispanics have already started moving into mainstream America. It is a move that they welcome in spite of having suffered hardships and pains at the hands of their onetime oppressor. They will no longer be treated as second class citizens.

In time, their political views will parallel those of the still powerful White majority. Their ranks will probably be sufficient in number so that the new White majority will reign long after the year 2043.

In time, what used to be White will no longer be White. The huge melting pot will operate as usual. In it will be Whites, Asian, Hispanics, and Latinos. The new

White race will take on a darker skin color due to mixing, but it will be preferred to a darker color resulting from adding Blacks to the mix.

Although they will not be as fair skinned as they once were, they will retain their racial identity as White. Consequently, it will be considered a small sacrifice to make in order to maintain their position of prominence in the social strata. Tanning salons may experience a decrease in business, and there will be fewer people lying around in the hot sun on sandy beaches, but the White majority will live on.

The United States will not be a country made up of multiethnic groups of which it had once welcomed with open arms. It will be a country made up of the brownish White majority that will emerge from the new melting pot. Then and as always, there will be the Black minority, a group that has never been willingly added to any mix.

White supremacists are hardcore about maintaining a White majority and keeping Blacks and other minority groups at the bottom—especially those of color. They strongly believe that the political and socioeconomic strata should be dominated by the White race.

They believe that the child born from an interracial relationship is more intelligent than the Black parent, but less intelligent than the White parent. Per capita, and coming from similar backgrounds, Black and White intelligence levels are the same. People who believe that there is a difference are people that hope there is a difference. They continuously reinforce their hopes with less than rational thoughts just to keep themselves believing that they are above all others.

What a person believes is reinforced by whom they communicate with. If a person believes in evolution, then most of their conversations regarding evolution will be with people that share their belief. The opposite is true for those that believe otherwise.

By communicating with people whose opinions and thoughts are similar to those of your own, you reinforce each other's beliefs. The same analogy can be applied to the belief by some that White people are more intelligent than Black people.

What would it take in order for some radical sect to overthrow the United States government and take this country back to slavery? They could not do it if their forces were comprised only of the radical sects that would join their coalition. It would have to be an all-out venture supported by the federal government.

The federal government may not always operate the way that the citizens of this country would prefer seeing it operate. However, it is impossible to turn the federal government against the people of this country with the goal of maintaining or establishing White supremacy. United States politics may appear to be shabby at times, but not to that extent. Consequently, no organization rooted in America will ever become formidable enough to overthrow the federal government—not for any reason.

Every race of people on earth seems to chide those that are not part of their race. When the Europeans settled in this country, they were welcomed by the Native Americans, yet Christopher Columbus declared that he had discovered a new world. It was new to him, but people were here when he arrived.

Those that were here first welcomed Columbus ashore; they were willing to share their country with Europeans and live together in peace. In time, they taught the new arrivals how to survive in a foreign land. After getting a toe hold, and having sufficient numbers, the new arrivals ended up slaughtering the Native Americans, took their land, and ended a way of life that would be no more.

When ethnic heritage in America becomes such that the race of the majority can no longer be determined by the color of a person's skin, then reason and logic dictate that racial hatred and inequality will end. However, political poppycock from those still living in the past and hoping for the return of the White majority will still have the need to know the dominant genetic traits of the population. They will want to know so that they can configure the people and put together the next racial divide to constitute a new majority.

DNA testing—or some new and improved method—will become the norm for determining race. New guidelines will have to be developed—what is the dominant racial trait and in which category does it fit on the scale of genetic variance. The data will be used to see whose genetic traits place them close enough to be included in the next White race of people that will not be White.

Should we be the civilized beings that we should be, then earth would be close kin to heaven. Yet, we cannot do that, or perhaps more fittingly, we do not want to do that. It seems like we're satisfied with things just the way they are—excluding the fact that the ratio of Whites to non-Whites is on the decline.

We must be satisfied, because we do little if anything to make things better. We talk about change, and things do change—it's inevitable—but who reaps the rewards, or the benefits, and at whose or what expense.

Not so long ago, White people would not sit in a restaurant with Black people—they didn't have to be sitting next to each other—they didn't want them in the restaurant unless they were cooking, cleaning, or serving. Today, it is not uncommon to see White grandparents or maybe great-grandparents walking around holding the hand of their racially mixed grandchildren or great-grandchildren.

When seeing them, one has to wonder if they have always been blind to Black and White relationships, or did they too at one time see Blacks as being an inferior class of people—how do they feel now that their bloodline has been permanently tarnished. Are they proud of their mixed blood grandson, or do they just tolerate him, because they are stuck with him?

It is a common sight, and one that is beautiful. They always appear to be proud grandparents, and every human being should hope that they are rather than looking and seeing and then wondering if what they see is real. When walking along together, it makes those that care feel good—like things are getting closer to where they should be.

If ten thousand kids just one year old and representing all races could survive in an isolated place completely void of adults, would they segregate themselves based on race? They most definitely would not. They would live together as a single unit in peace and harmony.

Children are not born with prejudices, they are not bigots, they are not racists, and they are not segregationists.

Those are the stupid things that they learn from us; we teach them and too many of us are too good at teaching the wrong things.

Suppose that two young men were placed in an isolated environment where they would be free to roam and wander at will. Suppose further that one of the men is a White racist and the other is a Black racist. Finally, suppose that they're left to survive in their isolated place of exile—alone or together, whichever they choose—for fifty years.

Since both are racists, back at home, they hated each other. Even in their new isolated environment—just the two of them—they still hate each other. However, they are both stuck in the same place for fifty years. They're free to hate and call each other names whenever they please without any reprisals … other than ill spoken comebacks from the other. They could fight, or one could even kill the other just to get rid of him.

A loner could survive—others have—but it would be much easier if they worked together. Working together means that there has to be dialogue between the two …

not hey nigger or hey honky, but, "Will you please help me with … ."

If two people spend enough time together talking and doing things to help each other, then eventually, whatever separates them becomes less important than it once was; it would probably even disappear. They would forget about the ill feelings and the ill spoken words of the past and create a bond of friendship that would be stronger than the wall of hate that kept them apart.

After spending fifty years together in some out of the way isolated place, they're rescued … returned to civilization. Would their way of thinking go back to what it was when they were young men, or would they maintain the feelings that they had for each other while in exile?

The answer to that question can be nothing more than a guess. We cannot isolate two people for fifty years for the sole purpose of answering a question,. However, we can offer a sensible response based on reason and logic.

Usually, we become more attached to the people that we are around the most. Whether related or not, they become family. Of course, that's not always the case—sometimes the people that we are around the most are those that irritate us the most—those that ask and never give back. Yet, we don't hate them simply because they're a pest or a pain in the … . We just stay away from them.

Today, people still segregate themselves based on an assortment of reasons, e.g., race or economic status. However, as always, there are exceptions. Most residential neighborhoods are pretty much segregated, but not nearly as much as in the past.

At one time in this country, Whites, Blacks, Hispanics, Asian, Chinese, etc. We're all separated. Each group had their own section of town. They lived there and they did most of their shopping there. Segregation was forced on some and with others, it was by choice. Many of those living in White neighborhoods—especially the middle class and upward still do whatever they can to bar minorities from living next door.

Generally speaking, Black people are not bothered by White people wanting to move into their neighborhoods regardless of class. Upper class Whites will accept an upper class Black family into their neighborhood, granted that acceptance may sometimes be merely a gesture of tolerance and void of good intentions.

Poor Blacks and Whites are prejudiced toward each other. Neither group wants to live near each other. Therefore, poor Blacks and poor Whites have but one place where they are accepted—in their own part of town.

I grew up on a farm in Tennessee. A White family lived within shouting distance of where we lived. Their adopted daughter and I were the same age. Whenever she had the time and if she saw me working outside, she would walk to our house just to be around me. She always seemed to feel very comfortable, but I wasn't.

Whenever she talked to me, I was always polite and I talked to her, but I was apprehensive—talking to a White girl in Tennessee. It was during a time when White and Black people still did not socialize together in the south. Her parents seemed to be as naïve about what was going on as she was. They didn't seem to pay any attention to what she was doing; I was the only one with any concerns.

During the fall of the year, the girl's father stopped by to talk to my parents. He wanted to know if it would be alright if I could come to their house and help their daughter with her high school homework. My father said that I could.

I arrived at their house at sundown. When I walked in, the girl's parents were getting dressed for church. They said that they would be leaving in a few minutes, but they would return around eleven o'clock pm. The girl had gotten her books and she and I were sitting on the couch together … sitting as close to each other as possible and her parents never said a word.

After her parents had left, we kept sitting next to each other and reading in her math book. I still remember the short green skirt and White blouse that she was wearing. Most of our time together was spent on math problems and how to solve them.

After we had finished with her homework, we sat and talked for a few minutes. After a while, I stood and said that I had to leave. She walked me to the door, and we said goodnight to each other.

I have never been able to completely understand how her parents could allow me to come to their house, and then, they leave us there alone. Had I made a good impression on them …

they trusted me that much? Were they of a new generation that felt differently about Whites and Blacks?

Apparently, the answer to at least one of those questions is yes. However, I wouldn't leave my seventeen year old daughter and a seventeen year old boy alone in my house at night under any circumstances. After thinking about it for so long, I had to come up with something to satisfy my mind... why did they leave us alone together at night?

Her parents are both dead, so I can't ask them. The only thing that I can do is guess. I have satisfied myself with an answer that I may not truly believe, but maybe one that I want to believe.

I have told myself that they left us alone, because they trusted me. Right or wrong, I'm satisfied with it. They can rest in peace, and maybe they had always been at peace; I helped her with her homework, and then I left. When they returned home, they found their daughter in the same condition as when they left. My only regret was that I left her alone in the house at night.

CHAPTER 13

TURNING AMERICA WHITE

IN THE UNITED STATES, WE have hate groups that would like to rid this country of its' mixed heritage and create an all-White society. The organization, Americans for Self Determination (ASD), believe that separation of races will be the civil rights movement of the twenty first century. They don't believe that it is possible for a multicultural society to function in harmony.

They believe that the diverse culture worked well during the early stages of this country's development, but it was due to the fact that the immigrants were all of European origin—they were White. The peace and harmony that existed then was interrupted when the mix included Blacks, Whites, Asian, Hispanics and Native Americans. According to ASD, tensions resulted because multiracial groups do not mix well.

Different ethnic groups probably mix better than ASD realize. The problem lies within one group—the White majority—exercising superiority over other groups. In the past, they have not given minority groups the full opportunity to mix with their group. In doing so, minorities have been forced into their own communities or neighborhoods.

The ASD is on target with the charge that peace and harmony was interrupted by the diverse culture of America. Yet, it is not because of Blacks, Asian, and Native Americans. Blacks were not brought to America with the intent of blending in and becoming part of any mix. They were brought here in chains for the sole purpose of being enslaved.

As slaves, Blacks were treated as cruelly as any people on the planet have ever been treated. There was an air of tranquility for sure. Yet, no one can possibly think that stooping and bowing and always maintaining a subservient attitude at the risk of being beaten half to death can be referred to as peace and harmony.

Like Blacks, Native Americans were never part of the mix. In fact, it is only by the grace of God that Native Americans were not wiped out completely—removed from the face of the earth because of greed. They were saved from complete annihilation, because someone came up with the idea of forced containment on reservations.

Asian were more like Blacks. They were the source of an abundant supply of cheap labor. White people had no more regards for Blacks, Native Americans, and Asian than they did a rabbit. They would kill either and think nothing of it.

Still, members of the ASD believe that it is impossible for a multicultural society to function in harmony. Their assessment is correct, and it has been proven. Yet, they blame the lack of peaceful accord on the people that have had to suffer most by the hands of an unjust majority.

ASD proposes that the United States be partitioned off into sections and each section to be occupied by specific races of people. Their plan is liberal enough to suggest that there be a section for those that don't mind living in an integrated society—indicative of the fact that they too realize that not all White people are segregationists or racists.

ASD believes that putting likes with likes is a must, because we have no other options since current political policies have failed. Their proposal is intended to bring about peace between the diverse cultures and to avoid the possibility of another civil war. However, it could be the first ingredient for another war.

Splitting the country into sections and segregating the people based on race would not be the right thing to do. Yet, it could be done if the federal government was in charge of the operation. The federal government would have to be in charge, otherwise there would be no divisions or sections within the United States—barring those that already exist as separate states but united. It would not be allowed.

Putting such a plan into action would put a mark on this country like nothing before. By necessity, it would be done with a political "I don't care attitude." Should it happen, it would probably be the first stage of a camouflaged backdrop of what's to come later—a political regime that the world has never seen.

Nonetheless, suppose that the country was divided into sections, and each section is to be inhabited by a specific cultural group. What process would be used to assign each group to a particular section? Should the decision be made based on popular vote, then White people would have the first choice simply because they are the majority.

Then, an election would be held for the other groups to vote on who would inhabit each of the remaining sections. Allocation of each section would require another round of voting until all sections have been assigned. As with the White majority, the most populated group would have first choice throughout the process of assigning the remaining sections.

The process would not be fair, but that would not be of much concern. People are used to it. One thing is certain, they would not draw straws, or use any method based on chance to assign locations. The group with the highest population would end up with the best parcel, and the smallest group would be the people that would end up living in Death Valley.

Popular vote would guarantee that the White majority has first choice. The process would be touted as being the only fair way of allocating each section, but it wouldn't be fair. Still, it would be the American way; Voting would let the people decide, but it would be a useless process. The people would know the outcome even prior to voting.

Realizing that they have been defeated, there would be some within each ethnic group that would relocate peacefully while others would not. The holdouts would be forced to move by the National Guard and the United States Army, which would be under the control of the White majority.

It would almost be the same process used to relocate the Native Americans when they had to travel the Trail of Tears. They would vow to provide military protection to all sections of the country whenever necessary. After settling in, people would probably stay on their side of the fence for fear of being shot if caught trespassing on the other side.

Forced segregation by the federal government would certainly be wrong. Should the government be willing to take such actions, it would mean that this country is probably getting ready for a real face lift—a completely new look. With the people separated based on race, it would be easy to do.

Suppose that White supremacist groups having agendas similar to that of the Aryan Nation were to merge with groups like ASD. All of the White people that wish to be separated from other races will have already been relocated to their own section of the country. They relocated because they don't particularly care for people of other races.

As time passes, their belief in White supremacy and White rule will no doubt become stronger, and so will their hate for other races of people. Their feelings and desires would be fueled by members of such groups as the

Aryan Nation. It would then be easy to get rid of everybody that lives outside their section of the country—all non-Whites and any Whites that chose to live in an integrated society.

The military would be composed of White segregationists. All non-Whites and any Whites wishing to live in an integrated society would have been dismissed from the military back when the country was first sectioned off. Then, the opportunity will be there, and it would be a good time to clean house—it would be a job for the military. They could get rid of any unwanted ethnic group in the country which would be all groups except the White supremacists.

When the operation ends, the United States would then be a country of White people. Those that had been relocated could return to their home place, or they might choose to stake off a place and live in another part of the country—the choice would be theirs. It would literally be a land of plenty.

The federal government would probably have a stronger hand in the affairs of both local and state governments.

With so few people in the country, there would be enough revenue to maybe settle the national debt—assets confiscated by the fed's following the massive slaughter and the elimination of so many social programs.

There would be a lot to do in Washington, e.g., amendments to the United States Constitution so that it reflects a single race of people, amendments to amendments that had been added to satisfy Black people and other ethnic minorities, sorting and burning documents that no longer apply, etc.

Truckloads of papers would have to be burned. There would be no need to keep scribed records that would be nothing more than reminders of the past. Statues and photographs of one time Black leaders would certainly be destroyed.

CHAPTER 14

A Subtle Approach

Cruel as it may be, it is possible to turn America White. It is true that there are several groups in this country whose agenda is to do just that. Each group has its' own ideas as to how to go about it. Some do not propose mass slaughter to accomplish their goal—preferring to be as subtle and discrete as possible. They are dedicated to making it happen, and they concede that it will be a slow process extending over a long period of time.

Some racially motivated groups see it as a process that out of necessity must start out small. Starting out small and progressing slowly would not attract attention. It will gain momentum with time as more and more White people join their ranks.

If left alone, they believe that it could eventually become an unstoppable movement. They would be left alone, because they don't propose breaking any laws. Their plan is to simply get Blacks away from Whites and keep them away.

Their strategy is to move into small southern towns—they see the South as being the area best suited to start, because a stronger racial divide is already present. A few Whites would move in and start buying property. Over time, the White population would increase, and subsequently, the Black population would decrease—theorizing that Blacks would develop a fear of so many unfriendly Whites taking over the town. Eventually, the town would grow and become almost, but preferably, all White.

Whites would work to get members of their group elected to local political positions, and then focus on state and federal offices. They see it as becoming a snowball effect—getting bigger and bigger as it moves along. The process would continue to expand until it covered the entire country. Unwanted ethnic minorities could go wherever they might want to go, as long as it was someplace away from White people.

Understanding that it would take a long time to accomplish their goal, these groups are willing to make the investment. Poor Whites will remain part of the new society and be treated pretty much as they are today. The ultimate goal is to establish White supremacy without going on a killing rampage.

Approximately two hundred and forty five million White people live in the United States, along with about forty five million Blacks. Consequently, Blacks are greatly outnumbered. In addition, White people are in control of the resources needed to conquer and reestablish the grim bygone era if they so desire. How many would be in favor and willing to participate is unsure. It could be a tough sell making such a radical turnabout in a country that is idealized as the epitome of democracy—in spite of its' flaws and misgivings.

It seems apparent that if White people are to maintain the White majority and reestablish White supremacy in the United States, then they must do it within the next thirty years. If predictions are correct, they will no longer be the majority by the year 2043.

Therefore, they cannot afford to institute a plan that is slow and subtle; it must be fast and consequently, it cannot be a covert movement. The unprecedented restructuring would have to be in effect while White people are still the overwhelming majority. For that reason, it is virtually impossible for a slow moving plan to be successful in weeding out minorities and maintaining a White majority.

CHAPTER 15

One World One Government

Should you believe what is written in the Bible, then you must believe that God mixed the paint, and then he created the multicolored rainbow of people that he wanted. Surely, many of those that want to rid the planet of its' diverse population are Christians. They attend church almost every Sunday.

They believe strongly in the Bible, yet they want to undo what their God has created. At the same time, they see nothing wrong with what they wish to do. They believe that the gates of Heaven will be opened when they arrive, and Gabriel will be standing there to welcome them in.

We live in a world that is constantly changing; we have different norms, different values, different ideals and different beliefs. We must realize that we did not come from the same mold. Thus, we are all unique, but being unique does not mean that something is wrong … we're just different. Yet, that is not good enough for some.

When considering all of the groups that have an agenda to maintain the White majority or to establish White rule, those that want to establish a One World Order are probably the most capable. Their goal is to install a one world government. If successful, the end result would be a way of life that the world has never seen.

Some speculate that plans have already been made for a super ruling power to take over. Should it happen, it will not be a government of the people and by the people, but a government by a chosen few that would apply to all. The supposed plan is to take over and rule the entire world.

According to conspiracy theorists, the New World Order will be led by powerful political figures and other highly influential groups and individuals. All countries of the world would be united as one, thereby eliminating regional and political boundaries.

Every human being on earth would be under their control and be subject to their rules and regulations. It would be rules and regulations drafted by the leaders and then presented to the people—not for them to give their consent, but for them to accept without any questions. Once the New World Order is in effect, the voice of the populace would not be well heard by those in charge. The self-appointed monarchs will rule with an iron fist.

The world would have a single police force and a single military force that would maintain law and order worldwide. Laws by which the people are governed will be few and simple, a speedy trial, no appeals, and swift punishment. The people would be unhappy, but crime would be almost nonexistent because of fear and the severity punishment.

Public opinion, wishes, and desires of the common people will be of little concern to the newly created government. Democracy will be replaced by absolute rule and authority. No one will question the modus operandi, and all will be unconditionally subservient.

A limited number of schools scattered about would educate the chosen few—those considered as having the highest potential to meet the government's needs. Hospitals and medical care will be limited—their primary purpose being to provide quality health care for the elite class only. When members of the working class become ill, some could be used as guinea pigs to advance medical science and technology.

The common people will have limited access to professional health care providers for minor ailments and superficial injuries. However, long term medical attention will not exist. Anyone suffering from chronic diseases will be allowed to die on their own terms—immediately by their method of choice or with assistance from professionals at the hospital.

For sure, the government will not spend money on health care for anyone when they are no longer capable of being an asset to society. Needless to say, not many will seek medical treatment for a runny nose or a hacking cough for fear of being diagnosed as having something more serious than a common cold.

Scientists predict that by the year 2100 there will be about ten billion people on earth—standing at the threshold of the plant's capacity to provide sustenance. If the New World Order took over the world at about the same time when the population reaches ten billion, the problem of overpopulation will be quickly resolved. Then will be the time when Black people can truly say, "The man is out to get me."

Racial issues will probably be as prevalent then as they are now. The people's resentment of government rule will be at an all-time high, but no one will complain—not openly out of fear. The man would be able to kill two birds with one stone. He could wipe out all of the Black people, along with any other non-Whites, thereby leaving a White society henceforth and for evermore.

The process of elimination could start in Africa by bombing and the dispensing of deadly biological agents. Naturally, there would be some survivors, but the military could go in and finish them off after the dust settles.

No entity on earth would be able to halt the operation, nor would there be any group capable of retaliation.

Although there would be no reason for the government to fear any reprisals from the people, the people outside of Africa would never know what has taken place. The news media would be controlled by the government, and they would tell the people only what they want them to know. Even without a covert operation, a one world government with absolute rule has no reason to hide, because in their world there would be nothing to fear.

Eliminating all Blacks in Africa in 2100 would wipe out more than a billion people, which would significantly reduce the world's total population. While they are at it, why not hit Asia as well and do the same thing as in Africa.

Such a broad act of extermination in Africa and Asia would result in the killing of millions of White people. Yet, the New World Order would know that in advance and would regard it as perilous fallout necessary to save and restore a dying planet. It would be viewed as not only being right, but necessary for the survival of mankind.

The first blow of death would be followed by foot soldiers to deliver the final blow. Their charge would be to get rid of any non- White survivors, and any persons afflicted with diseases, injuries or birth defects that might affect the wellbeing of the general public. In their wake would be a pure culture, free of those that had been labeled a burden on society and a disgrace to mankind.

It would be possible to keep secret the annihilation of millions upon millions of people on other continents. It would not be possible to hide the slaughter of so many living on the continent where the new world government is headquartered. People would be dragged from their homes and put to death. Only then will the citizens of the New World Order realize the meaning of democracy, and freedom; only then will some realize the struggles that Black people had had, why they were willing to fight and die to have what others had always taken for granted.

Wiping out every person that does not appear to be White will not guarantee a pure race of people. So many Whites have been tainted with the blood of Blacks—in some cases to the point where it is no longer visible—but medical testing will be available and necessary to make a positive and conclusive determination of race.

Today, DNA testing will determine a person's race. By the year 2100—assuming that is about the time when the New World Order might be put into effect—today's DNA technology will have become obsolete. It will have been replaced by some new testing method that is simpler and faster to perform.

Every person on the planet will be tested to insure purity of race. It will not matter which continent that he or she may be from. The only thing that will matter is that their genetic makeup does not contain any Black blood. It will be required that every newborn have tests performed to determine racial purity—just another safety measure to create and maintain an all-White society.

The declaration of the New World Order will dictate that any person appearing to be White, yet having a detectable level of Black genetics will be put to death. To the surprise of the ruling class, it might become necessary to change the requirement of no detectable levels of Black genetics to some acceptable level of tolerance.

Otherwise, the desired population of the plant might fall far short of their goal. However, that requirement will only be temporary.

Should it become necessary to accept a trace of Black heritage, it would be tolerated so long as it is not expressed to the point that it is visible. The person must appear to be White. Should any recessive Black gene be visibly expressed, that person—whether they be male or female and regardless of age—will be put to death. However, those individuals that are allowed to live, yet they carry the recessive gene, will be rendered sterile.

Every man, woman, and child will have a computerized chip—or some sort of non-removable data collecting and tracking device—inserted into their body. The government will be able to track the movement of each individual and maintain an up to date database on health, age, level of productivity, etc.

When the earth's population has leveled off at the desired number of inhabitants, the world leaders will initiate another culling process. They will go back and identify those individuals that carry the recessive gene of Blacks—those that had been spared. Eventually, any Asians, Latinos, and Hispanics that had been spared will probably go the same way as Blacks. Then the new world order will have a pure race of people that is all White.

Planet earth will never become over populated again. The number of children that a family can have will be limited. However, that number will be adjusted from time to time as necessary.

Although the ruling class will be the people of privilege, there is no reason to believe that they would be exempt when they are no longer an asset to their own creation. They will be allowed to go the way of the common people. Just like today, there will be someone waiting for another to succumb or to falter so that they can take their place.

Cemeteries will become a thing of the past. All of the dead will be incinerated and their ashes spread on some out of the way desolate area as required by law—thereby, eliminating any possibilities of contaminating the earth. Cremation will be an all-expense paid procedure taken care of by the government.

In the New World Order, all of society will be mere servants or working class citizens, save the privileged heads of state. The working class will serve each other by plying their skills toward producing durable and non-durable goods needed to keep society functioning. Each worker will be placed in a production role where they are best suited based on past experience. Of course, each will have the opportunity for advancement.

The economy will function in part like it did prior to the New World Order. The working class will consist of farmers, textile workers, hardware manufacturers, etc. Goods will be shipped back and forth between what used to be different countries. The method of payment for services rendered will require negotiation.

When the New World Order takes effect, there will be disagreement on how the new government should be formatted. Some already propose a single monetary unit while others believe that no monetary system should be required.

Society's working class will receive some type of benefit for their labors. If that benefit is not in the form of money, then it might be in the form of provisions, e.g., more food, a better quality of food, luxury items, etc. Whatever the case, a system of rewards will be necessary to enhance the quality of production and to stimulate creativity and innovation.

No individual will be allowed to own property—the government will own everything, including the people. Imagine earth as being one big plantation and all of the people as being slaves. It will be a reminder of the past, and every person living will get to know firsthand what it was like.

A New World Order of government would be the first regime to equal and then surpass the atrocities of Nazi Germany under the rule of Adolph Hitler. It would look a lot like Hitler, but it would include every country in the world with another Hitler in charge. It's frightening to think that any group of people would ever entertain such an idea. Yet, there are those that do.

The elderly would not suffer from the agonies that accompany old age. Instead, they would accompany the others that don't fit into the new society, or they could be put to death.

Undoubtedly, there would be some of different races that would escape the new government's attempt to rid the earth of their presence. Some might even be able to hide out someplace in the sparsely populated world and multiply, but their numbers would never increase to the point that they could ever become a threat to society.

Blacks and society's other unwanted minorities and misfits could eventually become the subjects of a new sport. They could be turned out and then become the prey to be tracked down and shot like animals. Imagine a game reserve where a person could buy a permit to hunt and kill society's rejects. It would be one of the amenities provided by the privileged ruling class.

Picture the parents in the new society taking their kids to the zoo for a day of amusement. The big draw would be a few human misfits—probably Blacks—naked and kept in cages like animals. Imagine people staring at them and tossing popcorn and other food remnants over the fence to see the half-starved sub-humanly treated beings fight over the crumbs.

Being White would not be an advantage over being Black or any other color. White people would be subjected to the same treatment as Blacks and other minorities when they become ill, step out of line, or when they are no longer productive for whatever reason. It would all come under the heading of population and disease control.

The New World Order's goal is to have a total world population that does not exceed one or perhaps two billion people. The Unites States Census Bureau estimates that the total world population today is a little over seven billion, but it will increase to about ten billion by the year 2100. That being the case, then the world population would have to be reduced by about eight billion people in order to meet the goal of the New World Order in the year 2100.

Should it happen, White and Black people would then get to know each other. They would learn to communicate, and to trust and understand. Maintaining a close bond would increase their chances of survival in a world where they are unwanted.

Society's rejects, especially Blacks, might be assigned another species name. They would probably be placed in the same classification as monkeys. It would be done, because they would definitely not be classified as human beings.

Society's misfits could even be relocated to Africa and turned loose to roam at will. The entire continent would be theirs and set up as a hunting reserve for those of privilege.

Killing, culling, and the reclassification of species would guarantee an entire world inhabited by one race of people, the White race. Then, it will be the end of the rainbow.

The big question remains, "Will a New World Order be implemented—if so, then when?" With so many news outlets today—including, Tokyo Rose—it's difficult to separate fact from fiction on a topic that could very well be true, or merely false beliefs by some that have done their research and then come to their own erroneous conclusions.

Conspiracy theorists tell us that the plans for a new world order were set into motion more than a hundred years ago. They claim that the major wars and the national and international political turmoil that we have already experienced have all been part of their agenda.

The turmoil in today's world coincides in part with their philosophy. Should it happen, a one world system of government could survive for a long time, but it is doubtful that such a regime could ever become permanent. When people get tired of being oppressed, then they revolt.

However, that's what the world is like today. For those who believe that a New World Order is on the horizon, they can see their plan coming together. For those that don't believe—it's nothing new—we just have some social problems that need to be fixed.

Edita: © EPBCN — Espacio Psicoanalítico de Barcelona
Balmes, 32, 2º 1ª
08007 Barcelona
93 454 89 78
info@epbcn.com
http://www.epbcn.com

1ª edición: Septiembre de 2015

Maquetación: Josep Maria Blasco y Carles Fabregat
Portada: Fabián Ortiz, Carles Fabregat y Josep Maria Blasco
Diseño de la colección: Josep Maria Blasco y Carles Fabregat
Depósito legal: B 20771-2015
ISBN-13: 978-1515120087
ISBN-10: 1515120082

www.ingramcontent.com/pod-product-compliance
Lightning Source LLC
Chambersburg PA
CBHW030437290526
45786CB00001B/333

* 9 7 8 1 5 1 2 3 9 0 4 7 6 *